50
Things to Do in
BABY'S FIRST YEAR

50

Things to Do in

BABY'S FIRST YEAR

The First-Time Mom's Guide for Your
Baby, Yourself, and Your Sanity

AMANDA RODRIGUEZ

ROCKRIDGE
PRESS

For general information on our other products and services or to obtain technical support, please contact our Customer Care Department within the United States at (866) 744-2665 or outside the United States at (510) 253-0500.

Rockridge Press publishes its books in a variety of electronic and print formats. Some content that appears in print may not be available in electronic books, and vice versa.

Interior Designer: Patricia Fabricant
Cover Designer: Julie Schrader
Art Producer: Janice Ackerman
Editor: Myryah Irby
Production Editor: Jenna Dutton

ISBN: Print 978-1-64152-914-3 | eBook 978-1-64152-915-0

R0

To every parent who finally understands that the struggle is entirely too real, but also entirely so worth it.

Contents

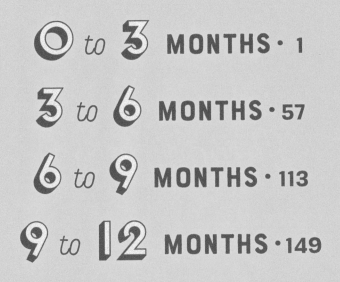

Introduction

Thirteen days after we were discharged from the hospital with our newborn, we found ourselves in the emergency room at midnight. The on-call pediatrician sent us in to make sure baby was okay after trying to make sense of a few of my harried calls. After a thorough exam, they declared our baby was perfectly healthy. What I described as "incessant projectile vomiting" was more of a spitting-up situation that had developed as a result of overfeeding. "Think about giving him a pacifier, Mom." That was the doctor's earth-shattering advice to calm my baby's desire to suck without giving him so much milk that he had to push it back out.

Fortunately, babies are resilient. He suffered no ill effects from this experience. I, on the other hand, spent hours attempting to curb the milk production his epic feeding sessions had inspired. On the bright side, getting my first scary mom moment out of the way in the early days did help me move forward with less anxiety and, before I knew it, I was changing diapers one-handed while getting dressed, eating breakfast, and feeding the dog.

I want to help you get there, too. You may have snatched this book up in hopes of getting there faster. I feel you on that urgency. You've been sent home from the hospital with not much more than a few minibottles of formula, a hat, and a bunch of pamphlets about cord-blood banking and baby life insurance—two things you're probably not thinking about right now because what you really need is for someone to teach you how to do the sleeping-baby transfer without waking the kid up. I got you, boo: Hold your breath, pause briefly after every movement, and say goodbye to rings, bracelets, and your Apple watch for the next few months, at least.

It will come to you. Some things are going to come easily, and some things are going to come from Google. Regardless, your body and brain will instinctively adjust to the day-to-day care and keeping of the minihuman you've been blessed with. Eventually, things like holding a bottle with your chin so that your baby can eat while you slam back a taco will feel natural. What doesn't come quite so naturally is remembering to care for yourself and your relationships throughout this journey.

WHAT TO EXPECT WHEN . . . READING THIS BOOK

I wrote this book as a mom who has been there—not once, but three times—as a teacher who has worked with kids from pre-K through college, as a newborn photographer who has taken photos of over a hundred newborn babies, and as a blogger who has written about my parenting journey for more than 10 years on my blog, DudeMom.com. I've shared my mom wins and fails on several other family and parenting blogs, have been featured in numerous parenting YouTube series, and contributed to a number of parenting books. If you live in the Baltimore or D.C. Metro area, you can often spot me on your TV providing parenting-related insights for local news segments. I've even spent time talking about mom life on the *Today Show* couch with Hoda and Jenna. (Special guest Maria Shriver noted how cute my shoes were!)

The point is, I was you once, sitting on my hospital bed, staring at the face of this magnificent little person, wondering if my baby belly would still be a thing come Christmas.

This book, organized in three-month periods, includes 50 helpful things you can do to simplify life with baby, and also make the most of it. It's a combination of expert advice, product recommendations, inspiration, and real-life storytelling that will inform you, empower you, and make you feel like a confident baby-care boss who can also appreciate balance. Because becoming a parent doesn't mean you're no longer a person. It's totally cool for you to have wants, needs, and relationships that require nurturing right alongside your baby. So yes, we'll cover stuff like getting more sleep and weaning, but we'll also talk about sexy time and when you can check out the new brunch place that opened down the street.

Ahhhhh, balance.

"Twelve years later the memories of those nights, of that sleep deprivation, still make me rock back and forth a little bit. You want to torture someone? Hand them an adorable baby they love who doesn't sleep."

—Shonda Rhimes

The big day has finally come!

Your womb oven is empty, and the baby you've been baking for the past 10 months is finally here. You can count those tiny fingers and toes and kiss those chubby cheeks you've dreamt about since you got that positive pregnancy test. Now the real work begins.

The awesome part is that you can mostly see your feet again, and your baby is even more perfect than you ever imagined. The not-so-awesome part is that your baby isn't the only one wearing a diaper home, and the hospital staff seems to have forgotten to leave your copy of *How to Parent Perfectly* on your bedside table.

Fortunately, neither of you will be in diapers forever, and that book doesn't exist. There is no one right way to do this, no magical parenting formula. There *is* a loving way to do this, and that's all you need at the moment. Focus on getting to know this new little human who has your heart wrapped tightly around their little finger, and get yourself healed up and healthy.

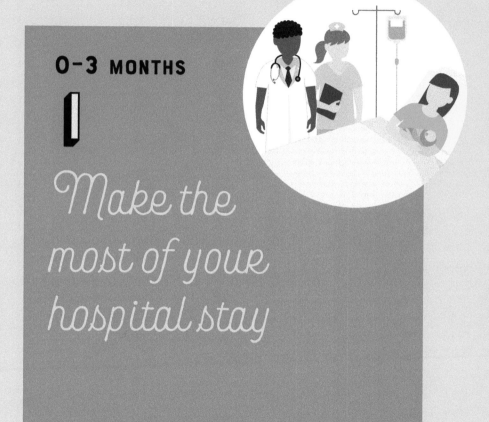

0-3 MONTHS

1

Make the most of your hospital stay

After what seems like 900 months of pregnancy, you're finally the proud parents of the most adorable and perfect baby human ever created! And. You're. Exhausted! Growing a human, whether you're the one doing the work or the one acting as support staff, is physically and emotionally draining. Throw in the birth experience and you could probably use a 72-hour nap before jumping headfirst into parenting. Not going to happen. But if you gave birth in a hospital, you do have the opportunity to take advantage of the care and wisdom the hospital staff has to offer.

The best bit of fresh-mom advice I got was to send the baby to the nursery. My mom told me that. It wasn't an option at the rooming-in hospital where I gave birth, but I did take every bit of free help and advice my nurses provided in those first couple of days.

For me, recovering from giving birth was an ordeal. The first time around I had a traumatic birth experience, and the second two babies were C-sections. I'll spare the gory details, but not only did I want the nurses' help with caring for my baby, I *needed* it.

Don't feel shy about asking questions, letting the nurses lend a hand, and practicing things like swaddling and umbilical cord care while you have people to show you the ropes. Also, try to spend time with the lactation consultant. For nursing moms, they are an invaluable resource to help you and your baby learn to perfect the latch and develop a healthy nursing routine before you leave the hospital. They may also be able to diagnose any potential issues before they get out of hand and provide guidance and support if you're struggling. If you're not nursing, lactation consultants can still help you understand the process of allowing your milk to dry up and advise you on how to deal with any early symptoms of engorgement.

Take advantage of every resource the hospital provides. And don't feel one ounce of guilt if you send the baby to the nursery for the night so you can get a couple of hours to sleep to recover.

AT THE HOSPITAL . . .

"When you give birth, your baby becomes a patient at the hospital. She will require medical care and testing as well. Here are a few things you can expect your baby to have:

* Antibiotic eye ointment to prevent eye infections that can result from passing through the birth canal

* Vitamin K shot in the thigh to prevent clotting problems

* Head-to-toe examination with vitals (pulse, blood pressure, breathing)

* Poop analysis. The nurse will want to see the color and consistency of the first few diapers.

* Jaundice checks (to ensure the liver is functioning well)

* Blood draw from the heel to check for metabolic diseases (such as sickle cell)

* Hearing test

* Daily weight checks

* Car-seat check at discharge. The nurse will wheel you out in a wheelchair and check to make sure you have a car seat that is properly installed."

—Meg Harrell, RN and owner of Megforit.com

2

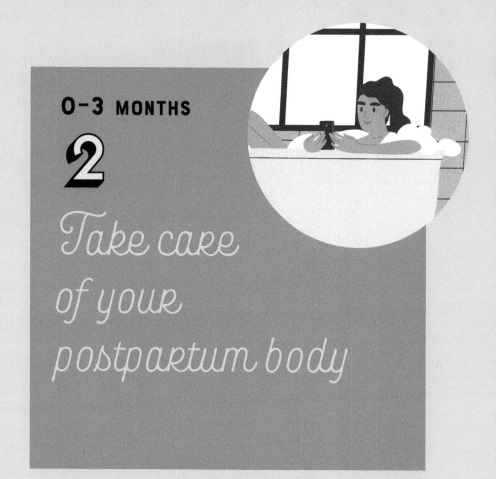

Take care of your postpartum body

Labor and delivery are two of the most naturally physically taxing events a woman will likely ever experience. Whether you had a vaginal birth or a C-section, your postpartum body is going to demand nearly as much attention as your new baby. Ensuring you're properly prepared and attentive to your own needs will lead to a healthier and more positive recovery overall.

IF YOU HAD A VAGINAL BIRTH, EXPECT YOUR NETHER REGION TO BE VERY SORE

If you experienced tearing or had an episiotomy, you can expect the pain to be a little more intense. After giving birth, few things felt more comforting than a sitz bath. I had no shame in my game when it came to sinking myself down into that plastic bucket to enjoy a nice warm soak several times a day.

Many women also find relief courtesy of a little warm-water rinse with the squirt bottle your hospital staff may leave beside your bed. Donut pillows to give you a little extra cushion while sitting may help, too.

IF YOU HAD A C-SECTION, PREPARE TO BE IN THE HOSPITAL FOR THREE TO FOUR DAYS AFTER BIRTH

And follow all of your provider's directions to the letter.

As hard as the simple act of sitting up will be, getting up and walking will be integral to your recovery. You'll want to get your body moving—and by your body, I also mean your bowels—as soon as possible so you can begin to enjoy real food again.

A cesarean section is a major surgery, and with it you'll have risks and side effects similar to other abdominal surgeries. Pay attention to your body, and don't expect to bounce back and hit the ground running. In fact, running will probably be off the table for several weeks. Don't feel like you need to push yourself.

TAKE CARE OF YOUR BREASTS

In those early days following birth, you're probably going to experience engorgement, which is when your breast tissue overfills with milk, blood, and other fluids. For those who aren't nursing, you should be able to rid yourself of this discomfort in a few days by making sure not to stimulate milk production. For nursing moms, expect engorgement to happen off and on until you and baby figure out a nursing schedule. It may also occur later if you skip a couple of feedings and don't pump to make up for it.

Other things that can help include wearing a supportive bra and using ice packs. When I was nursing, I fell in love with these nursing pad ice packs that fit easily inside of my bra. They didn't take long to freeze, and they were heavenly against my aching breasts. The Lansinoh TheraPearl 3-in-1 Breast Therapy Pack is a great option to have on hand.

TAKE CARE OF YOU

"Most women don't think about their own life after the birth, and many books leave out the reality of those days, weeks, and months after the baby comes. So, here are some pointers on how to survive, postbaby!

* Book an appointment with a physical therapist specializing in women's health and/or pelvic health. You will be thankful that you have put in the groundwork to heal your pelvic floor, and it will help you heal in many ways.

* Look for signs of postpartum depression. Hormonal changes will make your moods go up and down (especially in the first two weeks). Some days will feel amazing, and some days will be hard. Anxiety, changing sleep patterns, depression, tiredness, lack of appetite, and difficulty bonding with the baby are some of the signs of PPD and should be taken seriously.

* Slow down, don't think you can do everything, let people help you, and remember that these days are short!"

—Lindsey Welch, Bespoke Doula Services, CD, CBE

3

Take baby
to the pediatrician
. . . several times

The American Academy of Pediatrics recommends parents visit their pediatrician on the following schedule: three to five days following hospital discharge and then at one month, two months, four months, six months, nine months, and twelve months. Between well visits and sick visits, you're going to be spending a lot of time in your pediatrician's office this year.

I recommend keeping a journal to help prepare for these visits. Note things like how much and how often baby is eating, how much sleep they're getting, the number of wet and soiled diapers each day, and any other observations about baby's demeanor and habits. It's also a great place to write down any questions you have and to record the answers.

WHAT TO EXPECT DURING VISITS TO THE PEDIATRICIAN

Your doctor will perform a physical exam and check to see if your baby is meeting developmental milestones as expected. All of the measurements taken at birth—weight, height, and head circumference—will be repeated at each of baby's appointments to ensure healthy growth.

You can also expect your doctor to check things like how your baby's umbilical cord and circumcision, if your son had one, are healing. Your pediatrician will also be examining baby's development to be sure everything remains on track. Your baby may be able to lift their head a bit during tummy time, and you may notice baby is better able to focus on your face as well. Your baby may also be due for vaccinations.

GET READY FOR SHOTS

Your two-month visit will be significant because it is when most babies are due for their first big series of shots. Prepare to have as hard a time with that experience as your infant. This is usually a pretty hefty round of shots, so be sure to watch for side effects.

It won't all be sad, though. In addition to the inoculations, your doctor will be checking for fun things like baby's ability to coo and smile in response to others' faces.

10 QUESTIONS TO ASK YOUR PEDIATRICIAN

1. How do I know if my baby is getting enough food?

2. How often should I be feeding my baby?

3. Where can I get help with nursing issues?

4. How much sleep should my baby be getting each day?

5. How do I ensure they have a safe sleep space?

6. What can I do to help with fussiness?

7. Is their poop normal?

8. What vaccines do they need, and what side effects can I expect?

9. What developmental milestones should I be looking for at this age?

10. What behaviors or missed milestones should I be concerned about?

0-3 MONTHS

4

Take newborn photos

*T*hose sleepy, cuddly baby moments don't last long. The best time to capture them is when baby is fresh to the world.

Most newborn photographers recommend you take photos within the first week or two after birth. That's when baby is most likely to sleep and be maneuverable enough to capture those beautiful images we all ooh and ahh over.

Whether you're planning to book a session with a professional photographer or have your mom snap a few shots of you with baby, make sure this happens. Babies change so very quickly at this time. You'll want to make sure you capture those moments before they're gone.

IF YOU HIRE A PRO, SEE THEIR WORK FIRST

Most professional photographers have a website or social media channels showing off their work. Take time to peruse those.

Every newborn photographer is going to have their own style and approach to photography, and you want to make sure they're able to meet your expectations. If you're going for a particular approach, you should see evidence of that style in their prior work.

ASK UP FRONT ABOUT WHAT'S INCLUDED SO YOU'RE NOT SURPRISED BY THE COST

Many photographers will charge you a sitting fee that will get you in front of the camera followed by an edited gallery of beautiful images you can't have unless you pay more.

If you want to take your images and have them printed on your own, you want to be sure you find out, before your session, how much it will cost.

THINK ABOUT HIRING AN ON-LOCATION PHOTOGRAPHER

Anyone who has ever hauled a newborn into a department store photo studio will appreciate how challenging and unfulfilling such an experience can be for a new family.

Today, many newborn photographers are willing to pack up their gear and bring their setup into your home. They can capture beautiful images of you and your family in your own space, saving you the hassle of venturing out with your days-old baby and leaky boobs.

IF YOU DO IT YOURSELF

Pick a well-lit place in your home.

Light is one of the most important elements for capturing a good photo, and natural light is magic. So, pull back the curtains on your favorite window, plop baby in front of it, and snap away.

Choose a time when baby is full and sleepy. You'll be able to capture a couple of those precious, scrunched-up-baby sleep photos.

GET UP CLOSE AND CAPTURE THE DETAILS

You'll want to be able to look back on their tiny little hands, soft, round cheeks, and pouty little lips when they've grown into on-the-go toddlers who are terrorizing your house.

MAKE SURE YOU GET IN THE PHOTOS, TOO

If you're fresh off of labor and delivery, you may not be totally digging your new bod, but there is a unique beauty that comes with creating a life with your actual body. Celebrate it, capture it, and love it for the gift it has given you.

THE PERFECT NEWBORN SHOOT? GOOD LUCK . . .

"One of my favorite shoots included two panicking parents and a newborn who cried for the entire two hours I was there. They assured me he wasn't normally like that. I assured them that these things happen, and I wasn't worried. They were desperate to get the shots they'd been planning, but the moment they tried, his cries escalated. What these parents saw were tears, discarded props, and carefully curated outfits untouched in a pile on the bed. What I saw was emotion, connection, and lots of meaningful touch. We ended up with a gallery filled with kisses, tiny toes and fingers, and shot after shot of the parents cuddling their baby and comforting each other. Moments of peace as they leaned into each other, sleeping baby between them, and exhausted laughter as they realized he wasn't actually asleep and started crying again. A perfect reflection of life as first-time parents. Maybe your baby will pose like a champ in their sleep. But if they have other plans, embrace it. Your newborn photos don't just mark the life and details of your new baby but the life and details of your journey as parents."

—*Cindy Kane, Cindy Kane Photography, LLC*

5

Figure out breastfeeding

*I*f nursing is something you plan to do, the first few weeks are important to establishing a healthy feeding routine.

You hear so many women share how beautiful their breast-feeding experience was—how easy baby latched, how amazing and empowered it made them feel, how natural and intuitive it was.

Awesome.

The fact is that every mom has a different nursing experience. Some women and their babies pick it up easily, some of us require several tearful visits to the lactation consultant, some wind up pumping their magical milk essence into a bottle so baby can enjoy it, and others aren't able to go the breastfeeding route at all.

Here's what's true: Fed is best. As long as your baby is receiving healthy sustenance, you do you. Let the haters, naysayers, and soapboxers go on.

This is how it went for me with my first baby: His latch was terrible, I felt like his personal milk wench, and there was nothing natural about the next-level pain I felt every time Wolverine Baby—the nickname he earned from gnawing and clawing at my breast each mealtime—came at me wanting to eat.

Not a single thing was as easy as they made it look on those TLC shows. It wasn't awful, and I loved taking time away from everyone else to nurse my baby, but I still recall wishing I'd had more real info about what to expect.

BREASTFEEDING IS NOT SUPPOSED TO HURT

But sometimes it does.

There are countless reasons why you may be feeling pain while nursing your baby—improper latch, clogged ducts, mastitis, and sore, tender nipples, to name a few—and many of them are treatable.

Clogged ducts are usually painful, inflamed areas on your breast caused by poor drainage. This may occur when baby has an improper latch, you're wearing a poorly fitting bra, or you're not feeding regularly enough. Clogged ducts may lead to mastitis, a more severe inflammation of your breast that involves infection. Mastitis can be very painful and may cause you to feel quite ill. If you're having breast pain and/or develop a fever, you should make an appointment with your doctor.

Whatever the case, if you're experiencing pain while your baby is nursing, there's no reason to grin and bear it like I did—call your doctor or lactation consultant and make an appointment to figure out what's causing the issue.

YOU NEED A SUPPORT TEAM

In these first few weeks, you may regret your decision to breastfeed—the dry nipples, the nights spent nursing, the soaked nursing pads—and quitting may be a possibility you're seriously entertaining.

I looked to my partner and my mother for help when things got hard. You may turn to your lactation consultant or group, or to friends who have been there. There are so many resources available for nursing moms both online and in your community—you don't have to go on this journey alone. Reach out to the caregivers and other women in these communities.

DON'T BEAT YOURSELF UP IF IT'S NOT WORKING

Some women and some babies just can't make breastfeeding work. Low milk supply and other issues may come up, and there are those for whom nursing is not a good fit. If nursing isn't going to be a thing for you and your baby, forgive yourself and move on. Your kid is still going to love you, and you need to love you, too.

0-3 MONTHS

6

Get some sleep!

I'd love to sugarcoat this, but the level of exhaustion new parents experience shortly after baby makes the scene is no joke. There will be days when you'll do anything for a 30-minute nap. There will be others when, thanks to creative solutions, planning, and a lot of silent prayers to the baby-sleep gods, you'll be able to carve out some decent nights or afternoons—we're not picky here—of solid sleep. Here are things you can try to help sneak in more ZZZs.

SLEEP WHEN BABY SLEEPS

I know you want to shower and wolf down a few bites of the lasagna your parents dropped off, but it's time to prioritize. What's more important? A few solid hours of sleep, or food?

Okay, bad analogy. Because lasagna.

But you can eat a taco over baby's head while balancing a bottle with your chin as baby eats, too. This, however, is NOT a safe way to take a nap. As often as possible, shower and eat when you have someone available to tag team with baby so that you can sleep when baby sleeps and leave whatever else you can until later.

GET YOURSELF IN SLEEP MODE

I always struggled to fall asleep. The anxiety of knowing baby would be waking up soon often kept me from falling asleep until just before I had to pop back up to feed and change. To help with this, I made sure to set my room up for optimum sleep mode.

Black-out curtains and weighted blankets can be game changers for those struggling to get to sleep. I also invested in a diffuser to pump calming lavender essential oil into my room. You might also try a sleep meditation app. Calm, Slumber, Breathe, and Headspace are good ones to check out.

SKIP A FEEDING

Not baby, just you. If you have a partner who can pinch hit a few late-night feedings, or a relative willing to sleep over and lend a hand, make that happen.

Pick the one feeding that seems to be the most challenging and ask your sidekick to tackle that one on your behalf. It's a relatively simple switch if you're bottle feeding, but even nursing moms can pump and get in on this one. I waited until nursing was well established with my baby before doing this, but I can't even tell you how awesome it was to look at my husband with heart eyes in the morning after he took over the 2:00 a.m. feed. With him helping, I usually had time to sneak in a good four hours of sleep, a shower, *and* a taco.

SLOW DOWN ON THE CAFFEINE

Okay, don't panic. I'm not saying give up all caffeine. I'm not insane. However, coffee is a stimulant, and as much as we need it to survive the day, we don't want it leaking into our ability to chill. If your baby is on a strict wake-every-two-hours-and-terrorize-people schedule, having coffee coursing through your veins might make it tough to sleep when baby sleeps. Try to limit yourself to a cup or two a day, and don't beat yourself up if the day turns out to be a three-cupper.

DON'T SWEAT THE SMALL STUFF

Your baby won't be a newborn forever. Night feedings and wakings will be relatively short-lived. This, I realize, is only marginally reassuring when you're zombie-walking your way through each day. It may help to step back and evaluate what you're spending your time on, though. There are only two things that really matter for new parents those first few weeks: taking care of baby and taking care of yourself. You don't need to worry about meeting anyone else's expectations.

Your house is a wreck?
So be it.

Your roots need a touch-up?
Oh well.

You can't make dinner for your in-laws when they drop in for a visit?
And?

As long as you and baby are taken care of, everything else will still be there when your life has leveled out and you've got this new-parent thing under control. People who are really there to help will be lending a hand so you can nap and not taking notes on your performance.

7

Manage Mom and Dad

Having your own parents there to lend a hand when baby comes can be a true gift. My mother was by my side for the birth of all three of my children, and she has played a significant role in our lives every day since. I truly don't know what we would've done without her. That said, we did bump heads from time to time. Finding the best way to communicate, then establishing her role in our family was important early on. You may need to have a tough conversation or two with your extended family. Be sure you think through what that looks like before you jump in so you don't sever any relationships you cherish.

Be clear about what you want and need. Set up clear boundaries—like, we don't want anyone in the delivery room—and expectations—we expect you to call before you stop by—so everyone is on the same page. It's important that you include your partner in this discussion so that you agree on the role each family member should play. It gets frustrating for everyone when there are mixed signals.

Don't bother feeling guilty. It's normal to want to clarify the role your parents and your in-laws play in your children's lives. It's totally okay to set ground rules and expectations from the very beginning, and it's also okay if they change over time. You may think right now that you want Mom and Dad there for everything, then come to realize you'd rather go it alone a bit, or vice versa. Everyone involved should understand that this is a new and evolving experience, and adjustments may need to be made.

These conversations should start from the very beginning. When baby is born, many grandparents eagerly await the birth at the hospital. Some even find their way into the delivery room. If that's the birth experience you want, awesome. But if not, let your family know you'd like privacy. You're entitled to direct your birth experience however you want it to go without much concern for people who don't respect that. The same thing goes for when it's time to bring baby home from the hospital. As excited as your family may be to welcome you home, it's perfectly okay to ask them to give you a few days to settle in before coming over to greet baby. Remember, though, that as nice as it is to get to know your new little family member alone, it's also nice to have others to pitch in.

Your parents' new roles will take getting used to for everyone. They're not going to grandparent the way you parent—or even the way they parented you—and that's totally okay. They may need to feel out what they want this whole grandparent thing to look like. You can help by giving them a few guidelines and expectations. Meeting allergy protocols and abiding by your feeding requests are things you should stand firm on with grandparents who are pitching in.

Otherwise, it's okay to relax the reins a little. It's important to remember that grandparents are more than just glorified babysitters. Allow them the autonomy to make some decisions when they're in charge of baby care, and give them the leeway to develop a unique relationship with your child that everyone will one day grow to appreciate.

0-3 MONTHS

8

Celebrate baby's first milestones

At the end of three months, you'll be amazed at how much your baby has grown and changed. The soft, sleepy lump of baby you gave birth to will have grown into a gurgling, smiling, minihuman who is as in love with you as you are with them.

You'll be starting to see glimpses of baby's personality as you watch them learn to do things like smile, hold their head up on their own, and maybe even roll over. You'll be excited to share all of the new things baby is learning, and there are many ways to capture the moments and share them with everyone who loves you and your child.

SHARE ON SOCIAL MEDIA

If you have a private Facebook or Instagram account, these make for easy places to share updates and photos of baby. Some parents decide to start their children their own accounts, where they only post images and videos of baby so they can share them with selected people.

USE AN APP DESIGNED FOR PARENTS AND FAMILIES

There are milestone trackers, scrapbook apps, and photo and video apps geared specifically toward helping parents chronicle baby's first year and beyond. They allow you to have one central location where you can post all of your images and updates about baby.

Tiny Beans Baby & Family Album is one I've found to be super cool. It helps you collect, organize, and track all of baby's magical moments so you can cherish them and easily share them with friends and family. You can even make photo books from the images you save in the app.

MAKE A VIDEO

I'm sure you've seen time lapse videos before and, if you're like me, you watch in awe each time as baby grows from being a belly dweller to a high school graduate in a minute or less.

Time-lapse videos are a cool way to get a snapshot of baby's first year, and they are surprisingly simple to make. Ripl is an easy-to-use app for making videos from clips and photos. In a few clicks, you can create a video set to snappy music as a fun, share-able keepsake.

TAKE MONTHLY MILESTONE PHOTOS

There are tons of creative ways to make these photos memorable. Some people purchase (or make) monthly onesies to photograph baby in. Others create themed milestone cards with the baby's age to photograph alongside baby. The monthly milestone blankets you can easily find on Amazon are popular with new parents, too.

9

Survive
baby witching
hour

*F*rom about 5:00 p.m. until well after what used to be your bedtime, your baby has zero chill. Lots of crying and fussing, and nothing you do seems to make it better. Some of what you do seems to be making it worse.

We call it the witching hour, and it is as horrible as it sounds.

WHAT IS THE WITCHING HOUR?

Described as incessant fussiness without a clear cause, this experience is most likely to begin around two to three weeks postpartum. It usually lasts until baby hits the six-week mark. While all babies have their days, those experiencing the witching hours see more of a pattern—daily periods of inconsolable crying and fussiness, usually in the late afternoon and evening. Your baby may want to feed more or not at all and may seem extremely tired but will struggle to get to sleep.

WHY IS THIS HAPPENING?

Since newborns can't exactly tell us why they're so upset, we can only make educated guesses about what's causing baby to be so fighting mad every day. Doctors note a few things could be causing it—from changes in breastmilk hormones to the fact that baby life is hard, countless things are likely contributing to the struggle. The good news is that even if you can't determine the exact cause, there are things you can do to help restore calm to your day.

HOW DO I MAKE THIS STOP?

More than anything I wish I could give you a definitive answer to this question. I remember the days when I used to call my mom crying while clutching my screaming baby in my arms. I couldn't sleep, but I also couldn't eat or think when my newborn was screaming. I wouldn't wish that horror on any parent. Fortunately, all hope is not lost, and despite how it may feel, your precious little screaming nightmare baby won't always be this irritable. In the meantime, here are a few things that might help.

NURSE, NURSE, NURSE, NURSE, NURSE

For those with breastfeeding babies, you will likely notice that baby is constantly seeking the breast to soothe. It won't always work, but it's worth a try. Cluster feeding is a common reaction to the witching hour. Though it means you'll spend a few weeks feeling like a 19th-century milkmaid, this could lead to relief for both of you. Grab your headphones and your iPad, load up something bingeworthy, and focus on that while baby uses your breast as a pacifier.

NOT NURSING?

A pacifier works great. Hold baby close, give her the pacifier, and rock her a bit to help her settle. You may need to take a few trips around the kitchen to get her to calm down a bit.

AVOID OVERSTIMULATION

It's no coincidence that the witching hour tends to correspond with the end of the day. Baby has spent all day being played with, cared for, and doted on by visitors and she's basically had enough. Reduce as much outside stimuli as possible as your day starts to wind down. Ask visitors to wrap up their visits earlier in the day, push dinnertime back so you have time to relax with baby before bedtime, and think about adding a soothing nighttime routine to your evening.

TRY A MASSAGE

Infant massage can be quite soothing to your baby. Work it into your nightly routine, if possible, to help calm both you and baby. Johnsonsbaby.com has a great infant massage page with video and step-by-step guides to help make infant massage safe and soothing for your baby.

OTHER WAYS TO CALM

My babies were all suckers for warm rooms and white noise, so we used to sit on the toilet while Dad took his evening shower. The warm steam and the soothing sound of the water running helped calm them enough that they would easily drift off to sleep.

Other parents recommended taking a drive in the car, baby-wearing, skin-to-skin contact, white-noise machines or apps, and swaddling.

0-3 MONTHS

10

Watch out for the blues

The March of Dimes describes the "baby blues" as "feelings of sadness a woman may have in the first few days after having a baby." They are often also referred to as postpartum blues but should not be confused with postpartum depression, a more severe, long-lasting form of depression.

WHAT DO BABY BLUES FEEL LIKE?

The baby blues is a feeling of sadness that includes mood swings, crying spells, anxiety, and difficulty sleeping. It can begin a few days after giving birth and generally lasts a couple of weeks.

Women who experience it often report feeling overwhelmed or out of control and may even struggle to make decisions.

This is perfectly normal, and usually the baby blues will go away on their own.

HOW CAN I MAKE IT BETTER?

Though most women can expect to feel better a couple of weeks postpartum, there are some things that may help more quickly.

Self-care is an important part of regaining a sense of normalcy following childbirth. Finding ways to meet your physical, mental, and emotional needs will also positively impact your mental wellness.

Sleep is a great place to start. While it's difficult to get ample sleep as a new parent, it's worth prioritizing. Studies show that sleep deprivation severely impacts maternal mood. Combine lack of sleep with the change in hormones following pregnancy and the stress of new motherhood, and it's no wonder many women struggle to regain their mental/emotional footing on their own. When possible, push aside tasks like cleaning and laundry in favor of sleep or alone time, and think about streamlining tasks you must do to save time. Things like online shopping with curbside pickup can be a lifesaver to moms who'd rather spend their time catching up on ZZZs.

Don't think you need to be a martyr here. Asking for help doesn't make you weak or a bad mother. Attending to your personal health and wellness will allow you to be a stronger, happier parent who is better able to meet your child's needs.

So, take your friends up on those offers to help. Be vocal about what you need. Ask your partner to do a few feedings so you can grab a relaxing bath or use both hands to eat. Have your mother-in-law over to help you get dinner together for the night.

SHOULD I CALL MY DOCTOR?

Sometimes the baby blues is a little more than just a bit of postpartum sadness.

If you notice that your sadness is getting more intense, or that it is interfering with your ability to care for yourself or your baby, or if you start to feel like you want to harm yourself or your child, you should reach out to your care provider immediately. They can help you determine if you are suffering from postpartum depression and assist you in getting the help you need to overcome it.

Ask your partner to be on the lookout for warning signs that might indicate you're struggling. Even if you're feeling great today, the baby blues and more severe postpartum-related mental health issues can occur any time after you give birth.

This symptom checker might help them know what to watch for.

YOUR PARTNER MAY BE STRUGGLING WITH POSTPARTUM DEPRESSION IF SHE . . .

* Experiences sadness that gets worse or lasts longer than a few weeks

* Has extreme anxiety or worry

* Is acting withdrawn

* Changes eating or sleeping habits dramatically

* Misses appointments or forgets to care for baby

* Exhibits fits of rage very different from what she normally exhibits

PostpartumProgress.com is a great online resource for maternal mental wellness and provides countless resources for those struggling with postpartum depression and other mental illnesses related to pregnancy and childbirth.

0-3 MONTHS

11

Get back in the sack

$\mathcal{O}$ *r not!*

For those who have a partner in the parenting game with whom they have an intimate relationship, sexy time is bound to come up sooner or later. I'll be the first to admit that, while my husband was eager, sex was the furthest thing from my mind after bringing baby home. I was preoccupied with figuring out how my newborn worked and, after squeezing out a Honey-Baked-Ham-size human, I was a bit reluctant to test the waters.

Many women note a lower sex drive postpartum, while others are ready to get it on. The good news is that you're entitled to feel any type of way about hopping back in the sex saddle after giving birth.

WAIT UNTIL THE DOCTOR AND YOUR BODY SAY YOU'RE READY

New moms generally receive the all-clear at their four- or six-week postpartum checkup. If you had a vaginal delivery, doctors don't recommend any action before your checkup to ensure everything is healed up nicely, to avoid infection. For those recovering from a C-section, you need time to do just that—recover. As with any surgery, your incision needs time to heal before you partake in any type of physical activity, sex included.

IT'S NORMAL TO FEEL ANXIOUS ABOUT IT

Your body looks and feels different. Your relationship with your partner may have even changed a little. You have all kinds of hormones rushing around your body, and you're probably bone tired. Add the fact that you may have turned into a human milk machine, and you might still be rocking your favorite maternity underwear.

With all that going on, it's normal to feel anxious and apprehensive about being intimate with your partner again. If they can't understand that, they can take a walk. Seriously. Or a cold shower.

IT'S 100-PERCENT OKAY TO SAY YOU'RE NOT READY

Your partner should be understanding and supportive of your feelings during this time, and you should never feel rushed. At the same time, it's important to be considerate of your partner's feelings, too. They may be feeling disconnected from you and seeking a way to reconnect.

If you're struggling to find your way back to each other in the bedroom, have a frank talk about how you're feeling and what each of you needs to make it happen. Open communication is the best way to keep your relationship healthy, especially when you're both experiencing such a major life change.

YES, YOU CAN GET PREGNANT

Contrary to popular belief, you actually can get pregnant before your six-week checkup, and I have the siblings to prove it—10 months apart!

Some women won't get regular periods for months postpartum, especially while nursing. Even if you fall into this camp, you won't get much warning before you ovulate, and you could become pregnant before you even have your first postpartum menstrual cycle.

Make sure you speak to your doctor about your birth control needs at your follow-up appointment so you're protected, unless you want to risk having close-in-age siblings on your hands.

EXPECT IT TO BE DIFFERENT

Giving birth changes your body physically and emotionally. It impacts the relationship you have with your body and with your partner. It can even reconfigure elements of your internal anatomy. With all that going on, it's no wonder that postpartum sex is often a whole new world.

Remember, you don't have to jump right back in. Start slow and figure out what feels good and what doesn't. Intimacy can be felt in many ways. Even if you're not initially ready for intercourse, there are plenty of ways to spend time loving each other without going all the way.

LET'S TALK ABOUT SEX

"No one really talks about how hard it is to get your groove on after the baby arrives. Everything takes priority before sex: taking care of baby, getting enough sleep, etc. You'll have to make intimacy and sex a priority. The easiest thing is to lower your standards. Instead of long, passionate lovemaking sessions, slip in a quickie while baby naps. If you need more foreplay to achieve orgasm, read or listen to an erotic book as you feed baby or apply female stimulation gel right before your quickie. If your lady bits are still a do-not-enter zone, expand your definition of sex to more than penetrative sex. Think back to your high school days: making out, heavy petting, mutual masturbation, oral pleasure. Ultimately, be patient and listen to your body. Your sexual needs change throughout your life and what had you ready to jump your partner before baby may not work post-pregnancy."

—*Thien-Kim Lam, founder of BawdyBookworms.com*

0-3 MONTHS

12

Get out of the house

If there's one thing that most new parents can agree on, it's that new-parent life is exhausting.

Whether you're fortunate enough to have a helpful, supportive partner or even outside help, or if you're going it alone, adjusting to your new lifestyle as a parent will likely be emotionally, physically, and mentally draining.

That's why it's easy to fall into your "give up on life" pants, avoid the shower, and spend every day doing nothing more than keeping yourself and baby alive, especially once the novelty has worn off and your anxious-to-lend-a-hand visitors have started to peter out.

I struggled to find the confidence to take baby places alone. I guess I was anxious about all of the things that could go wrong, so I put off trips outside of the pediatrician and my parents' house for weeks.

I distinctly remember my first solo excursion out of the house with baby. I was going to Olive Garden for lunch with my mom. I was nervous that I wouldn't get the car seat in right, or that I'd forget something, or that baby would start crying the moment they delivered my fettucine Alfredo and I wouldn't get to enjoy it.

None of those things happened. The car seat worked perfectly, I had more diapers and wipes than I could use in a week, and the baby slept the entire time—because that's what three-week-old babies do.

For your own joy and sanity, plan ways to get out of the house and don't worry about getting a sitter. Young babies are usually two things: sleepy or hungry. Once you've slipped into a routine at home, you'll be getting a few hours of sleep at a time, and some of your own energy will come back. You'll also be better able to predict when your baby will be most needy throughout the day.

Plan an outing according to baby's sleepy time, and enjoy being out of the house.

GREAT PLACES TO GO WITH YOUR NEWBORN:

* **Brunch:** Make a reservation to avoid a long wait and plan it during baby's morning nap. Ask for a booth in a corner so you can feed baby comfortably if she wakes, but expect her to sleep through most of it.

* **Infant-friendly movies:** Did you know that many movie theaters offer midday, infant-friendly movie showings? The expectation is that babies may cry from time to time, so you can relax about being "that" parent and feel free to care for baby in the theater without hearing rude comments. Pro tip: If baby is inconsolable, you should probably step out anyway

to avoid disturbing fellow moviegoers and their sleeping babies, too.

* **Concerts and movies in the park:** If you have a summer baby, this is a great way to enjoy an evening out with your partner. If baby gets fussy, put her in the stroller and take a lap around the park. Be sure to settle yourself far away from the speakers so that baby's sensitive ears aren't overwhelmed by the sound.

* **Shopping:** They may not be in it for the long haul, but put baby in your sling as you take a lap or two around IKEA and she'll probably enjoy the ride. Bring a companion who can keep you company, take a turn carrying baby, or hold your stuff while you hit the restroom for diaper changes.

13

Think about babywearing

Babywearing is the ancient practice of using a sling or carrier to wear or carry your baby. It is a hands-free option that makes baby care more convenient for parents while also meeting your baby's need to be close to you often. If you haven't explored the idea of babywearing yet, now is a great time to familiarize yourself with the practice and determine if it's a good fit.

BENEFITS OF BABYWEARING

Parents who wear their babies report that it allows them to manage their lives more easily. It frees up your hands so that you can care for other children and complete household chores and errands. Babies who are carried also tend to cry less. They have their basic need for parental closeness met and can also regulate their breathing, heart rate, and temperature more easily.

In terms of your own physical health, carrying a baby around can be taxing on your body. I developed sciatica in my hip from constantly having a child flung to one side. Others have struggled with neck, arm, and back pain and injury as a result of lugging their babies around. Proper use of a baby carrier or sling can help reduce some of these strains. Choosing the appropriate carrier or sling for your baby, body, and activity will help make the experience more enjoyable for everyone.

CHOOSING A CARRIER

Wraps, slings, and carriers are all different options for wearing your baby. Each one has its pros and cons.

Wraps and slings, like Moby Wraps and Baby K'tan Wraps, are fabric-based options that require wrapping over and around the shoulders. They aren't structured—the area to hold baby and the straps for keeping it on are all created by wrapping the fabric strategically around your body. This option is ideal for very young babies. They can nestle into the fabric and don't need to keep their heads positioned any certain way. Slings can also be used more like a seat when older, larger children are able to sit up unassisted.

Baby carriers, like Ergo Baby, are more structured items with arm straps and leg holes. They can be worn in the front or on your back. Babies can be set in the carrier facing toward your body or outward so baby can see. They are a more ergonomic option and great for outdoor activities like exploring a city or taking a quick hike.

All of the options for babywearing work as long as baby is placed safely in the carrier according to the manufacturer's guidelines.

TIPS FOR BABYWEARING:

* **Choose a carrier that you can use easily**
Some carriers take a bit of practice, so don't get frustrated. But if you notice that you always require help getting it on or can't figure out how to get baby situated inside comfortably, it may not be a good fit long term.

* **You may want more than one carrier**
I wound up with three—one for around the house, one I shared with my husband for going out and walking, and another for when baby got a bit bigger. Buying new baby gear can get expensive, though. Fortunately, there are countless ways to find affordable items you need: Ask a friend to swap, visit a consignment shop or sale, look for them on eBay, or troll your favorite Facebook yard sale groups. Craigslist and local yard sales are also great ways to find high-quality, gently used baby gear for a fraction of the cost.

* **Give baby time to get used to it**
If you didn't start babywearing shortly after birth, baby may need time to adjust to the carrier life. Wear baby for short stints to start. Then, as she starts liking it, wear her for longer periods throughout the day.

* **Wraps and slings are easiest for breastfeeding mamas**
  They are less structured and easier to maneuver around so
  you can position baby safely to reach your breast while you're
  wearing her.

BABYWEARING BENEFITS

"Babywearing was a parenting game-changer for me. When my first
daughter arrived, it was a way for us to do things where a stroller wouldn't
work, like a hike. But it developed into so much more with each subse-
quent child. My girls struggled with reflux and wanted to be held and
upright. Not only did babywearing allow me to hold them and keep them
upright, it allowed us to be close to one another while carrying on with
other activities with their sibling(s). Babywearing by my third and fourth
daughters became our way of life. The bond that is created by having your
child so close to you is immeasurable. It also helps when you run out of
hands to attend to other children. A baby carrier is on my list of top 5
needed items for a new parent because it helps with a snuggly newborn
and helps with a toddler."

—*Krystyn Hall, writer and owner of ReallyAreYouSerious.com*

"Having children is like living in a frat house—nobody sleeps, everything's broken, and there's a lot of throwing up."

—Ray Romano

3 to 6 MONTHS

You've made it through the first three months with baby, and you have a lot of exciting things to look forward to in the next three months. Baby will start to do exciting things like roll over, eat baby food, and, best of all, sleep more through the night. So, say adios to sleep deprivation and go have fun with your baby!

3-6 MONTHS

14

Find your village

Whether you're the first of your friends to have a baby or one in a line of many, having a group of parents to connect with can help make the experience easier.

The Internet is an easy place to start. There are several online options designed to fill this void. Apps like Mom Life and Peanut focus on helping moms connect with other local moms. There are also numerous birth-month- and age-related Facebook groups to provide new parents with the opportunity to connect and share the journey of parenting.

Starting your own social channels and building your own following is another avenue. I started my blog, DudeMom.com, when my youngest son was a baby. As a stay-at-home mom to three young boys, I wanted to share our story and build a connection with other moms in the same stage of mothering. Plus, I needed to connect with others during the day while my husband was working long hours. I was able to use my blog and other platforms, such as Facebook and Instagram, to find support, share our story, and form friendships both online and off.

While I have truly enjoyed the connections I've made through my online platforms, I found the local, in-person mommy groups I joined to be immensely beneficial for both me and my baby. They were especially helpful in the early days, because they saved me from running to my pediatrician or relying on Google when I had questions.

Having the mom meetups on my schedule also gave me something to look forward to, encouraged me to explore my community more, and provided us both with much-needed face-to-face peer interactions. It was nice to put on real pants and go talk to other adults once in a while.

Note: I recommend not taking baby to any mommy-and-me groups until they've received their first round of vaccines.

If you're interested in finding a local new parents' group to connect with, your hospital or birthing center and your OB/GYN might be able to point you in the right direction. Your new pediatrician may also be a great resource. There are also several national groups, including MOPS (it's not just for moms of preschoolers, promise) and Mocha Moms (a national group for moms of color). You can visit their websites to find a chapter near you.

FINDING SUPPORT ONLINE

"Motherhood is beautiful, challenging, and rewarding, but it can also be very isolating. Facebook parenting groups that are run correctly by admins who do not allow drama and negativity give these new moms a place to go while their baby is asleep to seek out camaraderie and emotional support. It's a place where they can get advice when they don't know what to do or need reassurance that they are making the right decision. Most importantly, it is somewhere they can go to share their stories when they haven't been able to have an actual conversation with another adult all day. I wish in those early years of parenting that I'd had access to a Facebook group of thousands of supportive moms all over the world who understood what I was going through. The friendship and a place to belong no matter where I was or what time of day or night I needed it would've made motherhood a lot less lonely."

—Tiffany O'Connor, Founder of Boymom Squad
and HashtagLifewithBoys.com

15

Prepare to go back to work, or not

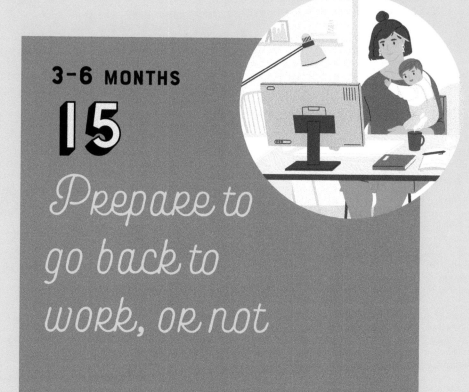

The World Health Organization recommends women be allotted 16 weeks of leave to recover from childbirth and care for their newborns. Unfortunately, to date, the United States only requires companies with more than 50 employees to allow women 12 weeks of unpaid leave following the birth of a child, with no requirements for smaller organizations. The U.S. remains one of the only countries in the world not to adhere to the World Health Organization's recommendation regarding maternity leave. The situation regarding paternity leave is similar. For those fortunate to have parental leave to take advantage of, many new parents are thinking about heading back to work around the 12-week mark. There are many logistics and emotions to muddle through when it comes to being a working parent or not. No matter which option you choose, you're going to find yourself struggling to adjust to your new normal.

SO, YOU'RE BECOMING A STAY-AT-HOME PARENT?

Awesome!

If you've made the decision to stay home full-time and do the baby-raising thing, you may slide easily into your role as full-time parent. Or you may be struggling. Giving up a career you loved and worked to develop is hard. Many parents who choose to stay home full-time find themselves dealing with quite an identity shift. Your status switch, from professional boss babe (or boss dude—I see you, stay-at-home-dads!) to kid-wrangler, may not fit you any better than your prebaby jeans right about now. And that's okay!

It's totally normal to face this type of an adjustment period and even to discover that stay-at-home-mom or -dad life is not your jam. If you're committed to making it work, look for ways to break up the monotony that daily baby care can bring.

FEED YOUR SOUL

Find ways to feed your own creative and intellectual needs so you don't get burned out on mom or dad life. You may not have much time to engross yourself in a book, write in your journal, or work on your Harley in the garage. But carving out whatever solo time you can is important to maintaining your sense of self.

TIME TO HEAD BACK TO THE OFFICE?

Maybe staying home isn't financially feasible, or maybe you aren't ready to leave your career or business to be home full-time.

Awesome!

The working-mom/stay-at-home-mom shame game is alive and well. You don't have time for that! Never let anyone shame you for being a working mom—you need to do what's best for yourself and your family. Whether you're excited about heading back to work or dreading it a little, there's likely going to be anxiety about managing the process. Take a deep breath, make a list, and figure out the things that are in your control.

TALK TO YOUR EMPLOYER

Communication is key to any relationship. Be straight with your employer about your challenges and expectations, and make sure you understand theirs as well. You should discuss things such as how to manage childcare and leave when your child is sick. If you're nursing, you may also want to ask about accommodations for pumping.

THINK ABOUT CHANGING YOUR SCHEDULE

A gradual return-to-work schedule might help you and your family if your employer is open to it. Telecommuting is an option you could explore as well, at least during the transition.

MAKE SURE YOUR CHILDCARE SITUATION IS STRAIGHT

The process of finding adequate care for your baby can be time-consuming and nerve-wracking. I don't recommend leaving it until late. Once your childcare is ironed out, do a test run: Get up like you'll need to on a regular workday, drop baby off, and then go spend a couple of hours taking care of yourself. It will give you and baby a chance to test out the new routine—with a side of precious alone time.

If you're anything like me, the first few months as a new parent will be spent trying to sneak a few showers and as many naps as possible in between keeping yourself and your newborn alive.

3-6 MONTHS

16

Start some routines

ventually I discovered that living in week-old, spit-up-stained sweats was not a viable long-term option. That's when I discovered the power of routine. Routine allows you and baby to move through the day in a more organized, predictable fashion, giving you a sense of calm and accomplishment. For us, it was especially helpful when it came to sleep.

DEVELOPING SLEEP ROUTINES

Around three months old, babies begin to have more predictable sleep patterns. This will allow you to create routines. Your baby will still be taking several naps each day, and they will be able to sleep longer stretches at night. By about four months old, many babies can sleep through the night without needing to eat. That said, your baby may need a little guidance to get to this happy sleep space. Setting up naptime, bedtime, and night-waking routines will help.

NAPTIME ROUTINE

Many babies this age are still taking three to five naps a day. Try to lay baby down awake but tired, and expect them to last anywhere from 30 minutes to three hours. Give baby ample space and time to sleep, and allow them to wake up on their own when possible. I recommend not letting the last nap of the day be longer than an hour so that baby is ready for a longer sleep period at night.

It is important, however, that baby is getting their naps in each day so they're not overtired at night. When your grandma says, "She's going to sleep tonight!" after a busy day of being passed around to relatives, she has no idea what she's talking about. Overtired babies are often more restless at night after an over-stimulating day. Newborns can't manage more than about an hour of awake time, and trying to keep babies awake will most likely backfire.

BEDTIME ROUTINE

At bedtime, you want to create a predictable routine that will send cues to baby's brain that it's sleepy time. It's less about what you do and more about the repetition of these actions. Start your bedtime routine about an hour before bed each night, and once you figure out what works best to calm your baby, do that every night before bed.

If you've found yourself with an overtired baby who is struggling to fall asleep and stay there, here are some things you might try:

* Swaddle her.

* Try rocking baby to sleep. The gentle motion of your swaying often helps lull baby to sleep. Putting baby in the swing, walking in circles around your kitchen, and a quick drive around the neighborhood could work, too.

* Keep the room quiet and dark—no TV for background noise.

* Download a white-noise app. Sometimes the shushing sound works.

* Feed her. Or try a pacifier. Sucking tends to calm babies. It doesn't have to be a meal's worth of food—a snack should suffice if she isn't hungry.

NIGHT-WAKING ROUTINE

While some babies are starting to phase out the middle-of-the-night feeding between three and six months, many are still waking up hungry. Make this nighttime feed all business. No playing, no lights, even skip the diaper change if you can. You want baby to understand that, if they're not hungry, there's no reason to be up. When they're done eating, put them back to bed and head to sleep yourself.

If baby is struggling to find a sleep pattern, there are countless things that could be disrupting it. Sleep regression—your baby's resistance to sleep because they don't want to miss anything—is common. Teething, illness, growth spurts, and feeding issues can also impact baby's ability to get into a sleep pattern. If you and baby are struggling, talk to your pediatrician about what you can do to help.

ROUTINES CHECK-UP

"With an eight-year-old, a six-year-old, and a newborn to manage each day, it has been hard to get into a routine. Here are a few things that have worked so far:

1. Taking morning showers to help me get a fresh start to the day and clear my mind
2. Pumping at least two to four ounces after feedings to create a milk stockpile
3. Meal planning for the week and cooking two meals at a time
4. Preparing clothes and lunch the night before to avoid being late (this is one is huge)

Life with a newborn is hard enough, but incorporating these practices has allowed me to keep my sanity!"

—*Shelly Tucker, founder of MomsWithTots.com*

3-6 MONTHS

17

Tame teething

*F*or many, baby teeth start making an appearance by around six months. Baby's juicy mouth and persistence to gnaw at things might be your first clues that teeth are approaching. For nursing moms, your earliest indication may be when baby clamps down on your breast while you're nursing.

Teething is a long and varied process for babies and their parents. Here are a few things to know and how to prepare.

WHAT TEETHING LOOKS LIKE

You've probably heard tales of fevers and fussiness when it comes to teething, but what teething actually looks like can be different for each baby.

According to the American Dental Association, teething babies may experience fussiness, general irritability, and loss of appetite. They may also have trouble sleeping and drool more than usual. What they shouldn't experience are fevers, bouts of diarrhea, or rashes—although sometimes babies develop a "drool rash" on the chest because of drool-soaked clothing. Be sure to keep a dry bib on baby to protect her skin.

WHAT YOU CAN DO TO HELP

My babies were all pretty agreeable teethers—a couple of teething toys were all they needed to find comfort for their tender gums. If you're struggling to find relief for your baby, here are some ideas that might help.

* Put a wet washcloth in the freezer for 15 minutes and then let baby suck on it. Do not leave baby unattended with the washcloth—this works best while you hold her.

* Gently massage baby's gums with your finger. Make sure your hands are clean and your nails are trimmed before you put them in baby's mouth.

* Let baby chew on a soft-bristled baby toothbrush while you hold it so she can't choke.

A word of caution regarding over-the-counter teething options containing the ingredient benzocaine: This ingredient, used to relieve gum pain and found in products like Baby Orajel, has not been approved for use in children under the age of two by the Food and Drug Administration. They also discourage parents from using homeopathic products to treat teething, as these products have been found to contain questionable amounts of belladonna, an ingredient not determined safe by the FDA.

WHEN BABY BITES

We didn't have much irritability or sleep disruption when my first son was teething. One thing we did have, though, was a biter, and his favorite thing to bite was my breast!

What to do when baby bites: Don't overreact.

As much as you feel like yelping in pain when your little wolverine goes after your already tender breast, try not to react much. Often, your baby is as eager to watch your antics as she is to soothe her achy gums. Instead of giving her the show she wants, gently remove her from the breast and use your grown-up voice to say, "No biting!"

Don't yell, don't sound overly sad or pretend to cry. Just give her a little eye contact and let her know this behavior is not allowed. Once she realizes that biting babies are hungry babies and Mommy isn't making this fun, she'll quickly move on.

18

Think about sleep training, or not

A few notes about sleep training.

Many parents start to consider sleep-training options around the four-month mark. There are countless infant-sleep professionals and pediatricians who provide advice and guidance for sleep training your baby.

YOU DON'T HAVE TO SLEEP TRAIN YOUR BABY

Whether you get on the sleep-training bus or not, your baby is not going to be a night-waking terror for the rest of your life. It may feel like an eternity, but like all other phases, this will be relatively short-lived.

When my infant was struggling with sleep, I read every word on the Internet about sleep training. All of my research taught me one thing: I could parent more effectively, more lovingly, and more joyfully with empathy and comfort. So, I decided to let my baby tell me what felt good. Some nights that meant he nursed himself to sleep, others it meant Dad rocked him for a bit before he drifted off. All of them left us feeling good about the relationship we were building with our little person.

Did my son have a hard time going to sleep without us for a couple of years? Yes.

Did he sleep in my room until he went to kindergarten? Also yes.

Did I spend hours regretting my choices and beating myself up over the entire thing? Nope. I decided that my own sanity and the general health of our family was what mattered.

But that isn't what worked best for my second son. We did a more traditional sleep-training method with him, and it allowed everyone in the house to get much-needed rest.

Do what is best for your baby and your family. I always tell moms that there are no *should*s in parenting—there are things that work for you and things that don't.

THERE IS NO ONE WAY TO SLEEP TRAIN YOUR BABY

If you need to help your baby sleep through the night, there are several methods you may wish to use. Most of us are familiar with some version of Dr. Richard Ferber's famous "cry it out" sleep-training technique. Instead of providing comforts like rocking or feeding baby to sleep, the "cry it out" method encourages parents to put baby to sleep awake and allow him to cry, offering only brief reassurances by patting and soothing without picking him up. This will allow baby to learn how to put himself to sleep as opposed to relying on parents to help. Over the years, his original method has received criticism for causing unnecessary stress among parents and infants and, as a result, many have adapted, updated, and reimagined his methods to fit more modern parenting ideas. Dr. Ferber himself made additional modifications to the techniques in his 2006 edition of the book *Solve Your*

Child's Sleep Problems. In it, he encourages parents to adapt his method to fit their own child, parenting style, and circumstances.

While Dr. Ferber's "cry it out" technique seems to be the most well-known sleep-training strategy, there are several methods to help your child achieve restful sleep.

If you're looking for an alternative to "cry it out," the no-cry technique explained by Dr. William Sears may help. In this method, Sears recommends that parents stay engaged with their baby as he transitions to sleep; help baby find comfort with nursing, rocking, singing, and any other strategies they find comforting. This is a more responsive, intuitive sleep strategy that many believe encourages the parent-child bond and which Sears believes builds trust between baby and his parents or caregivers.

Regardless of what strategy you employ, remember to keep your eye on the prize: Sleep, for everyone, without all the fuss, is the endgame; how you find your way there is up to you and your baby.

MAKE SURE EVERYONE IS ON THE SAME PAGE

Whatever method you decide to go with, it's important that you get all of baby's caretakers on board. You want baby to understand that going to sleep is not a tumultuous, unpredictable affair. It's a comforting, relieving, safe experience that she should want to have over and over again.

MAINTAIN FLEXIBILITY

This doesn't need to be bootcamp. It's totally cool to allow flexibility in your process and respond to baby's needs in the moment. Maybe baby is sick or teething. Maybe she was overstimulated from being handed back and forth between relatives all day. As long as you have a comforting, predictable bedtime routine in place, it's okay to take a break from the sleep-training manual, especially if it's not going well or if your child (or you) could use a change of pace.

3-6 MONTHS

19

Teach baby sign language

Baby may not be able to talk, but that doesn't mean they can't communicate. By six months, babbling and cooing will be as much a part of her vocabulary as crying once was. While words are still a few months away for most babies, sign language is a great option to make it easier to communicate with your child.

BENEFITS OF TEACHING YOUR CHILD SIGN LANGUAGE

Teaching your child to use sign language to express herself can help eliminate frustration and lead to more accurate communication between you and your baby. In the long term, studies have shown that babies who learn sign language acquire verbal language more quickly. They may even develop a higher IQ.

THE SIGNS YOU SHOULD TEACH

The form of sign language you teach your child is not going to get her American Sign Language certified. You're looking to give baby functional communication tools that help get her needs met. She doesn't need to tell you what happened in the last episode of *Paw Patrol*. She just needs to be able to say that she could use a snack. Once you've mastered the basics, feel free to move on to fun stuff.

Parents often start with the following five words:

EAT

MILK

MORE

DONE   **SLEEP**

Once you've chosen the words you'd like to begin with, it's time to get started. Here are a few tips to keep in mind as you start your teaching journey.

SIGN IT AND SAY IT

You are working on language development here. You want baby to learn not only the signs, but also the words they're associated with. Every time you sign something, say the words.

BE PATIENT

Babies require repetition to learn. The more you show the sign, the more opportunities she will have to make the connection and understand. Expect it to take several weeks for your baby to sign her first word after you've demonstrated it hundreds of times.

MAKE SIGNING A PART OF YOUR LIFE

This immersive language technique will help aid your child's language development in the same way that talking to them all day does.

LOOKING FOR A LITTLE GUIDANCE?

Baby Sign Language Made Easy, written by Lane Rebelo, founder of the award-winning Tiny Signs® baby sign language program, gives parents everything they need to teach their babies to communicate without tears. You and your little one will learn to communicate about everything that goes on in their world, while having fun and strengthening your bond.

3–6 MONTHS

20

Create a photo book

*I*n today's digital age, most of us have countless images of our children that we can pull up in a second—on a screen. But when's the last time you printed a photo? The ability to take good photos quickly and easily has given us the gift of great memories, but it has also changed the way we cherish those memories.

I love finding creative ways to preserve those memories outside of my phone. You probably don't have a ton of time to create a custom photo book, but there are great apps and websites that make the process seamless. Here are a few I love.

Pinhole Press is a great option if you have the photos on your computer. They offer various sizes and designs and are pretty affordable compared to more custom options. Once you upload the images you want, their software will fill in the book you select, eliminating the need to spend hours customizing the layout yourself. I recommend taking a good look through the book to ensure you like the layout and order of the images before adding it to your shopping cart.

Chatbooks is ideal if your photos are on your phone or in your Instagram account. They offer an ongoing photo-series option that automatically creates photobooks from the photos you have in your camera roll or social media channel. It's an easy way to set it and almost forget it because the app sends you a notification when your 60-image book is ready to be approved. Before you press send, you'll be able to eliminate the meme screenshots you sent to your best friend and any other images that aren't book worthy. Then they send you a snack-size photo book featuring 60 of your favorite recent pics.

PRINT IT OUT

"Babies start to recognize faces as early as four months, so it's never too soon to introduce them to printed photos of their loved ones. Printed photos allow your baby to exercise early fine-motor skills while avoiding screen time and ultimately building recognition of those who love him or her most. Plus, printed photos serve as a keepsake long past their early learning moments."

—Erica Stoeckeler, Pinhole Press

21

Reconnect with your partner

Welcoming a new baby into the house is a major life change that can throw everyone into a bit of a tailspin. You and your partner are adjusting not only to new roles as parents but also to new roles with each other. The baby can draw you and your partner closer in many ways, but it can also drive a wedge between you instead. Finding ways to connect, away from baby, gives you the opportunity to discuss expectations and feelings that may be a source of concern.

For most couples, one-on-one time after baby comes is rare, especially in the early days. Even if you've had the time and opportunity to sneak away, you probably haven't had the energy to plan a date or even peel off your favorite sweatpants. Now that baby has a routine and things are a bit more predictable, it's a great time to slip away and reconnect with your partner.

That doesn't necessarily mean you have to plan an extravagant getaway. You don't even have to leave your house! An at-home "getaway" with a nice meal and uninterrupted conversation time after baby has gone to bed is a great way to catch up with each other.

If you have the ability to go out, eat dinner made by someone else, catch a movie, or do something fun together, awesome! Get that on the schedule ASAP. If not, think about trying one of these creative ways to enjoy each other at home.

NETFLIX AND BINGE

You both probably have something you've been waiting to watch, so why not do it together? Pick a show to binge, and promise to watch it together—no cheating! It will give you something to chat about other than dirty diapers and feeding schedules.

GET IN THE KITCHEN

You have to eat, so why not make dinner prep a fun way to spend an evening together? Choose a new recipe, and prepare a late dinner together in the kitchen. You can pair it with your favorite wine and make a romantic evening out of it. If you like a little friendly competition, challenge each other to a cook-off or a bake-off to see who can make something better.

WINE AND PAINT

A quick trip to the craft store, a couple bottles of your favorite wine, and you have your own DIY paint night at home. Don't worry if your pictures come out terrible—the fun of doing something together is what matters.

GET YOUR SING ON

You may need to head to the basement for this one so you don't wake up baby, but a little at-home karaoke gets the blood pumping and the laughs going.

GO STARGAZING

This is a great summer activity that you can do right in your own backyard. Lay out a blanket, cuddle up, and gaze at the sky. The conversation will flow, or you'll drift off in each other's arms.

3-6 MONTHS

22

Don't obsess over percentiles

*B*y now you've taken baby to a few wellness visits with your pediatrician. They all start about the same way: Baby gets weighed and measured, then your doctor compares her physical accomplishments to those of babies her age across the nation.

Proud moms talk about their child being in the 90th percentile for height, while others worry that their child is in the low 20th when it comes to weight. I remember my son's head circumference being in the 30th percentile his first few visits while the rest of his body was hitting the 80th for both height and weight. I feared that it meant something was definitely wrong with his brain because it wasn't filling out his skull enough. Countless Google searches had me fearing for his life, and when I finally got the nerve to ask his doctor about it, he had a hearty laugh. My baby's head, his brain, and his entire body were fine. He was just having a growth spurt and was plumped up on breastmilk. Everything leveled out shortly afterward and he remains, to this day, about a 50th percentiler all around.

Those percentile numbers, growth charts, and milestones are meant to be a guideline, not the Holy Bible of child growth and development. It's important to keep them in perspective. Here are a few things to keep in mind.

PERCENTILE CHARTS ARE ABOUT GROWTH RATE, NOT SIZE

Doctors don't typically use percentile charts as a standalone measure. Measuring your child's growth and tracking percentiles is meant to note their rate of growth, not their size in this moment.

IT'S NORMAL FOR THERE TO BE SPIKES

Sometimes you go to the doctor and your baby seems a little beefy. Other times, not so much. That's totally normal. Young kids tend to grow in spurts, gaining weight and height quickly. My mom always used to say my kids grew out before they grew up because they usually put on a few pounds before they grew taller. A growth spurt, in weight or height, could throw off the percentile chart a bit, and there is usually nothing to be concerned about.

EVERY BODY IS DIFFERENT

The sooner you teach your children that, the sooner they will appreciate the skin they're in. The burden of comparison is one we've all grappled with. Middle school will be here soon enough; there's no need to set them on that path early.

IF YOUR DOCTOR ISN'T WORRIED, YOU PROBABLY SHOULDN'T BE EITHER

Your doctor is looking at the overall picture here: total nutrition, baby's growth rate, developmental factors, etc. They understand where your child is and should be when it comes to growth. That said, if you have a gut feeling something isn't right, trust it. I always tell moms to follow their instincts. They may lead you down a rabbit hole, but they rarely steer you wrong.

IT'S MORE ABOUT NUTRITION THAN SIZE AND SHAPE

As long as your baby is getting the proper nutrition overall and growing at a healthy rate, try to have some chill about their weight gain or lack thereof. Right now, your baby may be sucking down milk to keep up with her growing body or shunning it a bit in favor of fun things like rolling over and watching the dog play. Talk to your doctor about anything concerning, and don't get caught up in what the numbers say.

PERCENTILE PANIC

"A baby's size is determined by a lot of factors. Some is how well they're eating and some is possible illness, but much more has to do with genetics, heritage, and environment. It's not useful to get wrapped up in comparing your baby to another baby—unless they are identical twins being raised in the same home by the same folks. Percentiles are important, for sure, because they help medical professionals in two primary ways:

1. Is the baby in the range of normal for height and weight at any given time? It's a big range, for good reasons. If the child is below the (corrected for birth week) 3rd percentile or above the 90th percentile then we're going to watch more closely or try to figure out what's happening.
2. Is the baby following their own curves or jumping or dropping on the curve? If so, is it clear why? At certain points in development we expect babies to change curves, as they get more active, less interested in eating all the time, and more interested in other things like play or communication. Has a child been ill? In this way we do compare, but we compare that baby to that same baby last month or four months ago—that IS clinically useful.

It can be fun to write down, track, and even discuss the percentiles where your baby fits. But please remember—it often provokes anxiety in parents who are talking about this, or even parents who are just listening to others. If you're worried, ask your family doctor or pediatrician if you actually have anything to worry about!"

—*Deborah Gilboa, MD, AskDoctorG.com*

3-6 MONTHS

23

Survive baby's first illness

I hope well visits have made up most of your baby's trips to the doctor so far. However, as your child broadens their social circle or heads to day care, your baby will be exposed to germs. With their penchant for gumming down anything they can fit in their mouths, you can expect to see your first fever any day now.

I'm going to keep it real: Sick babies suck. Even a mild cold is hard to watch. They look so miserable, and it's not like you can toss them a DayQuil and tell them to sleep it off. My heart broke every time my boys suffered with an infection, even when it wasn't anything to worry about.

The tough part is that you usually just have to wait it out. There is no cure for the common cold, and it didn't respond to any of my threats of violence. The best thing to do is be prepared. No matter how much you douse yourself, your visitors, and your home with hand sanitizer, the average child will get about seven colds before their first birthday.

COMMON COLD SYMPTOMS IN INFANTS INCLUDE:

* Fussiness

* Fever

* Coughing

* Difficulty eating and/or low appetite

* Nasal congestion and sneezing

* Difficulty sleeping and excessive waking

If your child seems extremely ill or their symptoms seem to intensify, call your pediatrician.

WHAT CAN YOU DO TO HELP?

Comfort is going to be a big part of treating your baby's cold at home. She's going to be irritable and uncomfortable, but nothing makes someone feel better faster than to know they are loved and cared for. Expect to lay on the extra attention because it will probably make both of you feel better.

While you should never give your baby cold or flu medicines unless they're prescribed by your child's doctor, there are home remedies you can try that may provide relief for your sick baby's symptoms.

AT-HOME COLD RELIEF FOR INFANTS:

* **Elevate baby's mattress.** Use a firm pillow under a fitted sheet or wedged under baby's mattress. DO NOT allow baby to sleep on anything soft.

* **Offer food and fluids often.** If you have a bottle-fed baby, you may note that your child is struggling to eat and isn't finishing

what she normally does. For those nursing, you may note baby is spending a lot of time at the breast but is fussing and releasing her latch often. In either case, this is probably because her stuffy nose is making it difficult to breathe while sucking. Don't assume she's not hungry—give her plenty of opportunities to get the nutrition she needs.

* **Suction nasal passages before baby eats.**

* **Use a cool-mist humidifier in the room where baby sleeps.**

* **Only give a fever reducer if your pediatrician recommends it, and be very careful with dosing.**

* **Call your doctor.** If your baby is less than three months, you should make the call at the first signs of illness. For older babies, you may be able to treat a cold at home successfully, but call your provider if baby seems to worsen or doesn't improve within five days.

3-6 MONTHS

24

Make
" me time "
a priority

According to a joint survey done by HealthyWomen and Working Mother, 78 percent of moms report they put off taking care of their own health because they were too busy looking after their loved ones.

Moms aren't alone in this epidemic of self-neglect. A *New York Post* survey determined that moms and dads get only 32 minutes on average of "me time" each day. That's about how long it takes to pee, shower, and eat a couple of the Oreos I have stashed under the sink in the bathroom.

Parents are notorious for pushing their personal needs behind the needs of everyone else. But parenting takes energy. And not the kind of energy you get from the coffee you've reheated four times. Energy that allows you to parent with purpose and positivity requires more. You need to make time for rest, nutrition, fulfillment, and reflection—all things most parents are guilty of neglecting—and you never need to feel guilty or selfish for making time for self-care.

Consider the investment of time in yourself as a gift to your family. The well-being you get from meeting your own needs as a human is as meaningful to your family's care as any of the tasks you perform for them daily.

Make an effort to set aside time to slip away and recharge. Focus on something that will revitalize you and give you the energy to reorganize your thoughts and center yourself for the days to come. If you're like me and out of practice, these suggestions can help you find your way back to yourself:

MAKE IT SHORT

Don't overcommit yourself by agreeing to a big outing that will pull you away from baby for too long. The goal is simply to recharge. You can do that by retreating to your room for 30 minutes to journal or take a bath.

MAKE IT AFFORDABLE

Or free! As much as a monthly massage would make my life, self-care doesn't have to be lavish. It can be time to meditate or read. You're more likely to invest in yourself if you don't feel like it's a burden on your budget or your family. But splurge for that massage from time to time. Your baby-carrying back will thank you.

GET MOVING

It's amazing how a little exercise can help restore you in a short amount of time. If you can get out in the fresh air, it's even more therapeutic. No need to bust out a full sweat; a short walk around the block might be all you need. But getting the blood pumping for even 15 minutes is a great way to feel refreshed. Can't go outside? Check out Pop Sugar Fitness on YouTube. They have quick, fun workouts you can sneak in when you don't have time to get out of the house. Search for the 30-Minute Old-School Hip-Hop Grooves Workout on their channel—it's my favorite!

3-6 MONTHS

25

Interview sitters

*Y*ou're finally ready for a night out, but Grandma is busy. So is Aunt Lucy, Uncle Charlie, your college bestie, baby's godmother, and every other friend and relative who has been offering to pitch in with baby care. It's time to find a sitter.

Not to be confused with general childcare, we are talking about people you pay hourly to occasionally come to your home and watch your baby. The day will come when everyone who loves your baby is busy, or when you actually want to spend time with some of those people without baby.

Finding a reliable, capable, trustworthy sitter you can call in for these times is going to make your getaway more enjoyable. Here are some tips to help make that happen.

ASK SOMEONE YOU TRUST

Start with your relatives and friends who have older kids. They may be looking for a side job. A second option is to ask someone you know who has young children. She may have recommendations for sitters who have watched her own children successfully.

THERE'S AN APP FOR THAT

Care.com and Sittercity.com are two well-known apps that help parents locate quality care for their children. Whether you're looking for a full-time nanny or someone to sit with baby for a date night, these apps pair parents with trusted care providers in their area to simplify the process. You can do everything from setting up interviews to making payments inside the apps, and many even offer safety features like background checks.

FACEBOOK GROUPS

Another online option is your friendly neighborhood Facebook group. If you live in a community with a page, you can often find postings from people eager to add a little extra income through occasional babysitting. You can also take the initiative and post in the group that you're looking for a sitter. Generally, other neighbors will weigh in by sharing or tagging someone they've used in the past or know and trust. You may even get DMs from people who have someone to recommend—or someone to warn you about.

OTHER THINGS TO KEEP IN MIND:

* **The going rate for a sitter in your area may be a little steeper than you remember.** I was shocked to discover how much my 17-year-old sitter wanted. I was lucky if I pulled in $15 for the night watching three kids and a puppy when I was a teenager.

* **Your sitter should be at least 13, but you may also want to consider an older and more experienced sitter if you have a very young child.** Think about how overwhelmed you get when caring for your baby. Do you think a 13-year-old would be able to handle your infant for hours alone?

* **There could be tax implications if you hire a sitter or any type of home-based employee.** Educate yourself on these so you're not caught off guard come tax season.

Ready, Set, Eat: Start solid foods

*B*etween the ages of four and six months, both breastfed and bottle-fed babies will be ready to beef up their food repertoire with solid foods.

I found starting solid foods to be one of the most exciting things about new-baby life. It's thrilling to watch as they experience new tastes and textures. I remember looking forward to first foods for weeks before baby was ready! People said he'd sleep better when he started cereal, and I couldn't wait to see him make all the faces when he tried the peas.

IS BABY READY?

Age is one factor in whether your baby is ready to get her grub on, but there are other indicators as well. Look for these signs to determine if your child is ready to start her solid food adventure:

Baby is . . .

* Able to hold her head up for long periods of time

* Sitting up alone or with little support

* Interested in food

* Still hungry after nursing or a bottle

GETTING STARTED

Before you dive in fully, it's important to start with the basics—a couple spoonfuls of single-ingredient cereal mixed with a bit of breast milk or formula is an easy place to start. Doctors recommend introducing foods one at a time, over the course of a few days, to be sure your baby doesn't have any allergic reactions or sensitivities.

If you notice a rash, or if baby experiences diarrhea or vomiting, you should stop the food immediately and speak to your medical practitioner about next steps.

DIY BABY FOOD

As convenient as jarred baby food was, one of my favorite things to do for my babies was to make their baby food myself. If you want to try DIYing your own baby food, here are a few tips to help you get started:

* **Be sure you wash, peel, and pit any fruits and veggies.** You want to avoid choking hazards and make the food safe and easy for baby to digest.

* **Even things you normally might eat raw, like peaches and apples, should be steamed or boiled.** You don't need to cook bananas or avocado—they're already soft enough.

* **Use breast milk or formula to puree baby's food.** Do NOT use cow's milk.

* **Avoid salt and sugar.** Your baby doesn't need either to enjoy their food. Also skip the honey until baby is over a year old.

* **Consider baby-led weaning, the process where you allow your baby to simply enjoy various finger foods without pureeing or mashing them.** Many families find this a natural and simple way to introduce their babies to food.

SOLID TIPS

"**Introduce lots of foods and flavors:** Expose your baby to as many foods and flavors as you can in these first several months of eating solids. She'll likely hit a picky patch when she's a toddler. The more foods she's eating before she hits that phase, the more foods she'll eat as she goes through it.

Ignore the grimaces: If your baby makes a screwy face after a bit of broccoli, don't assume she doesn't like it—or won't eventually come around. Research shows parents give up too soon on foods and flavors. Respect your baby if she doesn't want another bite in that moment, but keep serving that food at future mealtimes.

Let your baby make a mess: An important part of starting solids is exploring the way food feels, looks, smell, sounds—and squishes between the fingers! Spread a wipe-able mat under the highchair, don't stress about the mess, and let your baby experience food with all of her senses."

—*Sally Kuzemchak, MS, RD, RealMomNutrition.com*

*"I've conquered a lot of things…
blood clots in my lungs—twice… knee
and foot surgeries… winning
Grand Slams being down match
point… to name just a few, but I found
out by far the hardest is figuring
out a stroller!"*

—Serena Williams

You're probably feeling like you've finally started to find your groove. Baby is sleeping and eating like a boss, and you've had time to master things like eating one-handed and dealing with a stage-five diaper blowout. High-five yourself and get ready to tackle alligator-roll diaper changes and escaping from your baby's nursery at night without being seen. Some call it parenting; I call it making magic. Abracadabra, y'all.

6-9 MONTHS

27

Time to babyproof

Whether she's rolling across the carpet, doing some version of crawling, or pulling up and cruising along the furniture to get from place to place, your baby has likely figured out a few ingenious ways to get what she wants in her hands. If she hasn't, your time is coming. Most children will hit this independent-movement phase between six and 10 months. Once your child is no longer a blob forced to lie where you leave her, she is going to be exploring every inch of your humble abode, and by exploring, I mean putting pretty much everything into her mouth. To keep baby safe, you're going to need to babyproof your house.

WHAT IS BABYPROOFING?

Babyproofing involves making your home environment as safe as possible for your baby. It may include restricting your child to areas deemed safe by your standards, removing harmful items so they're out of reach, and installing products to make your home safer for children.

There is no way to ensure your environment is 100-percent safe, but there are a number of things you can do to reduce your child's risk of injury. This room-by-room guide is a great place to start.

AROUND THE HOUSE

* Make sure window coverings are cordless, or use safety cord pulls to keep the strings away from baby.

* Add outlet covers to outlets.

* Anchor furniture to the wall.

* Place fragile items and objects that could fall on baby out of reach.

* Cover sharp corners on furniture. Roving Cove, a product that wraps around sharp edges, can be found on Amazon and is the perfect solution.

* Make sure cabinets and drawers can't be opened to prevent access to unsafe products as well as pinched fingers. I liked the magnetic locks as opposed to the latching options. They made finger pinches less likely, and grown-ups in the house didn't fight with them.

* Add door pinch guards to room doors.

* Place cords behind furniture, out of reach.

* If you have stairs, install gates at the top and the bottom of your staircase. These should be walk-through gates so they can't be pushed over.

IN THE KITCHEN

* Push counter appliances back, and make sure cords are up on the counter.

* Skip the tablecloths.

* If you have knobs on the front of your stove, get knob covers so baby can't turn it on.

* Get rid of refrigerator magnets that are small enough for baby's mouth.

IN THE LIVING/FAMILY ROOM

* If you have a fireplace, baby should not be able to access it. You can use a baby gate to keep your child away from the area.

IN THE NURSERY

* Keep crib free of pillows, soft blankets, and bumpers that could be used to climb out once baby is mobile.

* Make sure the slats of your crib are no farther apart than 2⅜ inches (6 centimeters). It should also not have a drop-side rail.

* If your floors are hard, add a plush carpet to help cushion falls should baby figure out how to escape the crib.

IN THE BATHROOMS

* Add nonslip mats to your floors and inside your bathtub.

* Remove medicines from lower cabinets, and check that they all have child-safety tops on them.

* Remove cleaning products from lower cabinets and other areas baby can reach.

* Install a toilet lock.

IN THE LAUNDRY ROOM

* Make sure baby can't access your laundry area. Keep the door closed, and only allow baby inside with you.

* Keep all products on a high shelf.

* Keep front-loading appliance doors closed at all times.

OTHER TIPS

* If your anxiety won't chill or babyproofing seems daunting, feel free to reach out to a professional. The International Association for Child Safety maintains a database of professionals here: iafcs.org.

* Add the number for poison control to your cell phone: (800) 222-1222.

6-9 MONTHS

28

Deal with
separation anxiety

*H*as your baby suddenly begun to cry when you drop her off at day care? Has it gotten hard for you to go to the restroom without her panicking? Your baby may be suffering from separation anxiety.

On the bright side, this is totally normal for babies this age. Doctors say that babies between the age of four and seven months come to understand the concept of object permanence. This means that before when you left their sight, they assumed you didn't exist. Now when you leave the room, they know you're out there without them, and they want you back, immediately. Basically, it's the science-y way of saying they miss you and they want to be with you. Awwww! It's kind of cute to know they love you this much.

Not cute? Their little hands clutching for you as the tears stream down their adorable little faces. Having to double-team them with the day care provider as you pry their hands from your hair. Discovering that it's not a mom urban legend—you really won't pee in peace again for a good five years. It's a whole thing, and it will turn your heart inside out.

While you may not be able to hurry this phase along, how you respond may make it short-lived. Believe it or not, this child that can't get enough of your face will be expertly ignoring you at middle school drop-offs before you know it. Here's how to get on the path to freedom.

LEAVE LIKE YOU MEAN IT

No running back and forth for extra hugs; no canceling your plans because your baby is sad. Say goodbye, give hugs and kisses, tell them you'll return, and then roll out. You don't want your child learning that their tears will make you do what they want.

TAKE IT SLOW

Give your child time to warm up to new faces before you hand them over. They're already going to feel stressed out when you depart, so you want them to trust the person you're leaving them with. If you're starting a new day care, spend time there together and leave them for a short period the first couple of times. If you're hiring a new sitter at home, have the person come over a couple of times before you have to leave for real.

DON'T TRICK YOUR BABY

She trusts you. If you want that to continue, lay off of the tricky disappearing acts. Don't ask someone to distract your baby so you can sneak away when they aren't looking or tell them you'll be right back and then leave for hours. Every interaction is an opportunity for your child to learn, and you want them to learn that it's okay to stay in this safe space until you come back for them. Disappearing suddenly and being dishonest about your return time teaches baby she can't take her eyes off you, or you may leave and not come back for ages. Making good on your promises teaches her that it's okay to be here, Mom will be back for me, and I can trust her. That's what you want to stick.

Most children grow out of separation anxiety without any type of medical intervention, but if you feel like your child is having a uniquely difficult time, something else may be going on. Bring it up at your next well-baby visit to see if your doctor has any insight.

SMOOTHER SEPARATION

"Separation anxiety in babies is perfectly normal, but there are ways that parents can help ease their little one's anxiety. If you are putting your baby in day care, plan on staying for a few minutes extra so that you can introduce them to the room and the fun toys, along with the caregivers that they will be spending the day with. It's also helpful to bring a comfort item for them. You could even sleep with the item a few nights so that it has your familiar scent on it. Lastly, when you are reunited with your child you can say something like, "Here I am, I came back like I said I would," with the same positive tone you did when you left. It helps them start to understand that you might leave but you always come back."

—*Alicia Peiffer, mom of three, preschool director, and author of MakingTimeForMommy.com*

29

Work on those motor skills

*A*s genius as you think she is, your new baby won't be penning her memoirs anytime soon. But she is probably eager to get moving. You can help her get on the pathway to independence by providing her with plenty of opportunities to develop her motor skills.

Motor skills are placed into two categories: gross (or large) motor skills and fine (or small) motor skills. Gross motor skills are those that involve the large muscles of your body, like your legs and arms and torso. These are needed for things like crawling, walking, running, and throwing. Fine motor skills involve smaller muscles of your body that allow you to do things like use a fork or spoon, write, and cut with scissors.

Babies tend to develop their gross motor skills ahead of their fine motor skills, which explains why your child may be pulling up and standing before she is able to use a spoon accurately. My first son took his first solo steps shortly before he was 10 months old. He was running around the house and climbing on the back of the couch well before his first birthday. Some of this has to do with genetics and body composition, but there are things you can do to support your child along the way.

GROSS MOTOR SKILLS AND ACTIVITIES:

* **Get out the toys.** When baby is enjoying tummy time, get her to practice moving by placing toys just out of her reach. She may not be able to get them at first, but the act of trying will help develop her muscles. Before you know it, she'll be scooting and squirming her way to what she wants.

* **Stand and jump.** Around the four-month mark, your child will be able to hold her head up unsupported. This is a great time to exercise those legs. Hold baby around the waist and stand her on your lap. She will probably figure it out on her own, but if not, play a game or sing a simple song while bouncing her up and down.

TOYS THAT HELP

There are safe products and toys for baby that help develop motor skills. Activity gyms—mats with toy-filled arches that hang over baby's head—are a great option to help with development. Babies will work to reach the items while on their tummies and on their backs, allowing them to develop different muscles. Infantino makes a highly rated option.

FINE MOTOR SKILLS AND ABILITIES:

* **Play Pat-a-Cake and Peek-a-Boo.** These activities help your baby improve hand-eye coordination as she learns to mimic your movements.

* **Keep small toys and books around.** Smaller toys, like blocks baby can hold in one hand and manipulate, develop fine motor skills. Board books that have cardboard pages she can turn but not tear also work.

TOYS THAT HELP

Melissa and Doug has a number of toys that promote the development of fine motor skills from a young age. Wooden puzzles with handles on the pieces are a great place to start. Baby won't be able to put them together for a few months yet, but she can practice picking them up and putting them in her mouth, a decent way to spend an afternoon when you're eight months old. Bead mazes, shape sorters, and stacking toys are also great ideas.

6-9 MONTHS

30

Get back to your workouts

I realized quite early in the postpartum game that my snap-back wasn't going to happen. Never again would I have the flat belly and firm thighs I had prebaby. Regardless, I quickly got fed up with being outrun by my crawling infant and decided that I needed to up my physical fitness game.

Despite all of the indicators that I needed to get moving, I've always had trouble finding motivation to exercise. Fortunately, I was able to find creative ways to make fitness more desirable for me as a new mom.

WORK OUT WITH BABY

My kid was already over 20 pounds by the time he hit the six-month mark, so he made the perfect medicine ball to help me get ripped. I Googled "home mom-and-baby workouts," and the results came rolling in. There are tons of these at-home workouts. Working out with your adorable baby dumbbell is way more fun than having Jillian Michaels scream at you and your core, and baby will probably enjoy it, too. Looking for one to start with? Check out Body Fit by Amy and Fit Mix Mom on YouTube. If you prefer a calmer fitness routine, try mom and baby yoga. Your local studio might offer it, but you can also find a ton of videos online.

WORK OUT WITH FRIENDS

What's even more fun than working out in your living room with baby? Working out with baby *and* your friends. If you're fortunate enough to have friends with babies who live nearby, think about setting up a Saturday morning walking date. If not, look to join a local moms' fitness group like Stroller Strides. They have these all over the country, and they're a great way to meet other moms while getting in shape.

WORK OUT AT A GYM WITH FREE DAY CARE

Is the thought of a baby break enough to pull you into a Zumba class? Sign up for a gym that has free babysitting and then go get your dance on, girl! It's a fun, liberating way to get your body moving.

A WELCOMING WORKOUT

"When I first returned to the gym after my fourth child, I was 38, still nursing, and struggling with postpartum depression. My doctor suggested a gym membership. Money was tight, but we bit the bullet—knowing what a bite that membership was taking out of our budget was a motivator in itself. I had not put on as much weight with my fourth as I had with my second and third pregnancies, but this time I was carrying a different kind of weight—the weight of shame. As I crept into the back row of the group fitness classes, I quickly found which classes were the welcoming and warm supportive environment I needed to inch my way back, one bicep curl and grapevine at a time. Fitness isn't how you perform on your best day—it's how you perform on your worst day. It's about showing up anyway—no matter what. You aren't showing up for the workout. You are showing up for yourself and what your fitness means to those who love you, need you, rely on you. Do it for them. They need you to be well. They need you strong."

—*Amanda B. Strand, founder of Freedom Group Exercise*

Plan a
getaway

Baby is sleeping through the night now, she's had a number of her vaccinations, and she can go longer between meals. It's a great time to plan a little family getaway! Whether you're going on a long weekend or visiting family, planning your first getaway as a family is going to be different from the way you planned when a couple's weekend was on the agenda.

THINK ABOUT HOW YOU'LL GET THERE

Traveling with baby can be overwhelming. Put effort into planning ahead so you and baby can have an enjoyable trip.

IF YOU'RE PLANNING TO FLY . . .

* **Fly direct if you can.** Getting on and off the plane with baby can be a bear.

* **Choose to fly when baby is most likely to sleep.**

* **Feed baby during take-off.** It helps relieve the pressure in their ears that could make them uncomfortable.

* **Preboard only if you don't have assigned seats.** Otherwise you're stuck waiting for everyone else to get situated.

* **Take your stroller to the gate for checking.** They will deliver it to you on the jetway when you deplane.

* **Consider buying baby her own seat.** Lap-held babies under age two fly free, but if you can afford it, the extra space might be nice—and you can bring baby's car seat along. Both the American Academy of Pediatrics and the Federal Aviation Administration say the safest place for baby during a flight is in a child restraint system.

IF YOU'RE ROAD TRIPPING WITH BABY . . .

* **Think about leaving at night.** It's cooler for summer road trips, and baby might spend most of the time sleeping.

* **Ride in the back with baby.** Spending hours with nothing to look at but a mirror will get boring quickly.

* **Don't overdo it.** Listen, your seven-month-old is not about to be a road trip warrior. She will need frequent breaks when she's awake, so plan them into your day.

* **Get a few new toys for the trip.** They might keep baby's attention a little longer than the things she plays with every day.

PICK A BABY-FRIENDLY DESTINATION

Baby-friendly is dramatically different from kid-friendly. You don't need to plan a trip to Disney your first time out. You don't need any special programming or food options for baby. Kids require space and entertainment and menus your infant doesn't. What you will need are accommodations that are appropriate.

For the sake of your fellow travelers, you probably don't want to take baby to a romantic B&B.

PACK SMART

It's easy to overdo it when you're packing for your first getaway with baby. Of course, you'll need all of the essentials: diapers, clothing, wipes, and such. In terms of gear, think about the things you know you'll need, and then see which of those items the hotel can provide. They might have a Pack 'n Play or crib you can use in your room. You may be able to rent a stroller for a day at your destination. Or a baby carrier might do the trick. If you're driving, you can pack your car with whatever baby needs. But if you're flying, plan to travel with the necessities and then purchase things like extra diapers, baby food, and other disposables when you arrive.

6-9 MONTHS

32

Start brushing teeth

There may only be a couple of teeth in there, but it's time to get on baby's oral hygiene now. Baby may not need to bust out the floss, but it's good to get into the habit of caring for her teeth before she has a mouthful.

CARING FOR BABY'S GUMS

Pediatric dentists recommend that parents clean baby's gums after feedings. This will help prevent bacteria growth that could damage teeth. Simply use a clean, damp cloth and wipe them off when baby is done eating. You can also use a silicone finger brush. Using these tends to serve a double purpose—not only does it keep baby's oral hygiene game in order, but it also feels pretty awesome on baby's sore gums while they're teething. My kids would sit on my lap and gnaw on my finger in that thing for ages.

CARING FOR BABY'S FIRST TEETH

Once your baby's first teeth come through, the American Academy of Pediatric Dentistry notes that it's important to start brushing baby's teeth with fluoride toothpaste to help fight cavity-causing bacteria. You only need a tiny bit to clean those first teeth, and you don't need to worry about rinsing. Use your finger brush or a soft baby toothbrush. Try the Jordan Step 1 Baby Toothbrush. It's short with a ring handle to avoid poking and choking.

Other things you can do to protect baby's teeth and promote good oral hygiene:

* **Never put baby to bed with a bottle.** When children go to sleep with milk in their mouths, the sitting liquid feeds the bacteria in baby's mouth and can cause tooth decay. If your child falls asleep while you're feeding her, softly wipe out her mouth before you lay her down.

* **Don't put juice in baby's bottle.** Even watered-down juice isn't great for baby's teeth.

* **Give baby a pacifier.** Not only are they soothing, they can help prevent thumb sucking—a habit that could be an issue later when their permanent teeth come in.

* **Involve baby as much as possible.** You have many years of brushing for your child ahead of you, but you want her to learn and understand why this needs to be done. Get baby involved in the process from an early age so she develops the healthy habit of brushing and tooth care.

* **Go easy on the sugar.** Babies don't need added sugar to enjoy their foods. Don't sprinkle sugar on any of the things you feed her, and try to avoid sugary foods.

FIRST DENTAL VISIT

"Pediatric dentists like to see babies before their first birthday, but their first appointment doesn't need to be the real thing. The goal is to get children comfortable with visiting the dentist. Take them with you on one of your cleaning visits so they can see everything is fine and nothing is scary or painful. Have them sit in your lap and ride in the chair. Take them to the pediatric dentist and do the same thing. Let them see how easy it is so they know they don't need to be afraid. On the first 'real' visit, your baby's dentist will probably just count her teeth and talk to you about tooth and mouth care, but it's still important to go early so your child begins to understand that oral hygiene and visits to the dentist are an important part of her overall health and wellness."

—*Maria Staroza, Dental Assistant*

33

Make mom friends

I loved being a stay-at-home mom, but there were times when I felt pretty lonely. I was young, so many of my friends were still single and working. We'd just moved across the country, leaving most of our friends behind anyway. I had been doing the stay-at-home-mom thing for a year, in a new city, and my husband commuted more than an hour each way to and from work. The only human I had to hang out with—or even talk to—was my baby. I was desperate to make mom friends. But it's easier said than done.

Whether you're a working mom with little time for socializing or a stay-at-home mom like me, you may have to be strategic. Fortunately, a little planning, a little plotting, and a lot of small talk could lead you to the mom friend of your dreams. Plus, even if you're on the shy side, your baby makes for an awesome icebreaker.

GO WHERE THE MOMS GO

Playgrounds, children's museums, libraries, Target—you have to hit up the places moms frequent with their kids if you want to find locals to connect with. Visit spots where everyone's children are in view so you can see who might be a good match. Once you're there, be friendly—smile, make eye contact, and strike up conversations.

USE TECHNOLOGY

Facebook groups are an obvious and easy option, but there are also apps for moms looking for mom friends. Peanut, dubbed "Tinder for moms," allows you to basically swipe right on the moms you'd like to hang out with. Mom.life, another app for moms, helps women connect online. The cool thing about starting your mom tribe online is that you can get to know each other before an in-person meetup, weeding out people who might not be a good match.

CHECK OUT THE DAY CARE MOMS

Their kids are the same age as yours, and you can get a sense of who the friendly moms are from the drop-off/pickup small talk. Once you think you've spotted someone you (and your kid) might find fun, start casually and ask if they'd like to meet up for a playdate. You can visit an indoor playground with your little ones to test the waters.

34

Start traditions

*W*hen I was a child, every Christmas Eve, my mom would let my brother and me open a little gift. We'd have clam chowder for dinner and then get into our Christmas jammies, climb on the couch, and watch It's a Wonderful Life together. When it ended, she'd give us our gift and we'd open it. Usually it was something for us to share, like a board game, but sometimes it was something small we each wanted. I looked forward to that tradition every year, and it was one of the first that I started with my kids when we celebrated our first Christmas together as a family.

Traditions like these are what tie us to our family and culture by creating a sense of identity and strengthening the family bond. They're a way to teach values and pass on your heritage to your children. They also allow us to create special moments and memories that are unique to our families to be cherished in the future.

I'm sure we can all think of family traditions we want to encourage around holidays, but traditions aren't only to be celebrated once a year. Traditions are really just purposeful rituals you practice the same time or same way repeatedly. They can be a part of your everyday, too.

For example, another childhood family tradition was eating dinner together each evening. It was important to my parents that they had this time with us every day. They would change dinnertime to accommodate work and activity schedules so that the four of us could make it work. It is not a tradition that I practice with my own family, but it is one that I cherish.

As you start your own family, talk to your partner about what traditions were important to them growing up and those they'd like to see your family practice. Share the ones important to you. Even if you weren't a very traditional family, there may be some that you'd like to start in your own home to make your child's life special in a new way.

FUN FAMILY TRADITIONS TO START BABY'S FIRST YEAR:

1. **Family dinners.** Maybe weeknight meals won't work into your schedule—that's cool. Try making Sunday dinners a special thing instead.

2. **Special birthday cakes.** Lots of parents celebrate baby's first birthday with a special cake, but think about making it an ongoing tradition. My son started getting donut cakes for his third birthday and has had them every year since.

3. **Saturday morning pancakes.** You can make them with baby in the kitchen. As she gets older, it can be something you make together.

4. **Collecting snow globes.** My family loves this one. Every time we visit a new location, we buy a snow globe. Growing up, my mom did the same thing with magnets.

5. **Buy matching holiday jammies.** Matching family designs are available from places like Target and Hanna Andersson; it's pretty easy to find a set you'll love.

6. **Watch a holiday movie.** Your baby may not be into it yet, but it's okay to get on the couch, cuddle with baby, and enjoy one with your partner. *It's the Great Pumpkin, Charlie Brown; Peter Rabbit;* and *The Polar Express* are all great options.

7. **Annual family photos.** A family I photograph does them every year on their child's birthday. For added awesome, they always include a four-foot-tall stuffed giraffe so they can note their daughter's annual growth.

STARTING TRADITIONS EARLY

"One thing that tends to get overlooked the most is being intentional about creating traditions with your little one right from the start. One of my family's most meaningful traditions is putting up our Christmas tree the day after my husband's birthday in December. It doesn't matter if it's the middle of the week—we pick out the tree that day and put all of the decorations on it. Even the baby gets involved, and we let them put ornaments wherever they want. It's something we look forward to every year, and of course we take tons of pictures.

Although it may seem like your baby is too young to remember or care about the time you put into creating these traditions, it helps to start early. Family traditions are an amazing way to build a sense of security in your children."

—*Brandi Riley, founder of MamaKnowsItAll.com,*
author of Just Us Girls: A Shared Journal for Moms and Daughters

"I rescind my early statement,
'I could never fall in love with a girl
who regularly poops her pants.'
(I hadn't met my daughter yet.)"

—Dax Shepard

9 to 12 MONTHS

You're quickly heading into the home stretch—baby's first birthday is on the horizon. It's hard to believe the sweet newborn you could hold in one hand has morphed into this wiggly, on-the-go fireball of fun and independence. She's got tons more to do over the next few months, and she has every intention of doing most of it before noon.

9-12 MONTHS

35

Get an adjustment

Have you ever been to the chiropractor? Postpartum chiropractic care has several benefits for moms who've given birth, but even partners, adoptive parents, and other caregivers can find benefits in a little postbaby adjustment.

Hormones get a bad rap—100 percent they're to blame for this adult acne I'm battling at the moment—but they also play a huge role in the building and birthing of your baby. They are responsible for the softening of your ligaments that allowed baby to make her way into the world. Unfortunately, that softening can lead to pain and discomfort for mom. From stress caused by added weight gain during pregnancy to changes in your gait and posture from carrying your bundle of joy from place to place once she's born, your body has been through the wringer in the past year or so.

WHAT DO CHIROPRACTORS DO?

Chiropractors diagnose and treat mechanical conditions. They are most concentrated on the spine but may also focus on joints and soft tissues. Chiropractors utilize hands-on spinal manipulation and a variety of other alternative-care therapies such as electrical modalities, massage, and rehabilitative exercises to provide pain relief.

WHAT CAN A POSTPARTUM ADJUSTMENT DO FOR NEW MOMS?

No matter the difficulty of your pregnancy, your child's birth, or even your postbaby snapback, you're going to note differences in your postpartum body. You may be all the way in love with your new bod, but that doesn't change the fact that it has undergone physical changes that can impact your daily life. A visit to your chiropractor can help alleviate ailments women continue to experience postpartum, such as sciatica, headaches, and back pain caused by changes in your posture. Chiropractic care can even relieve stress and anxiety, help strengthen weakened immune systems, and improve flexibility.

BEFORE YOU BOOK AN APPOINTMENT . . .

I spent many years in pain because I was afraid of the urban legends I'd heard about quack chiropractors setting up shop in storage units and paralyzing people, or worse. Pro tip: Never see a doctor in a storage unit. But also, do your research. Chiropractic care is extremely safe for the vast majority of patients, and negative outcomes resulting from procedures performed by well-trained, licensed chiropractors are rare.

Chiropractors do not typically provide quick fixes. It can take several visits to feel relief, and you may have to try a variety of treatments before you find one that works. Your chiropractor will work with you to find a treatment plan, and care is covered by most insurance.

Chiropractic care may not be a great fit for everyone. There's a lot of touching in spinal manipulation, so if that's not your jam, you may find it initially discomforting like I did. If it does provide relief, you'll likely find that the awkwardness of having your doctor lie across you to manipulate your spine is totally worth it. But, should you find the whole thing to be not awesome, you can stop going and chalk it up to your crunchy-mama phase. No harm done.

To find a practitioner who might be a good fit, ask your OB/GYN for a recommendation. You can also look to your neighbors, local friends and family, or community pages on Facebook and Nextdoor.

ADJUSTING TO ADJUSTMENTS

"Pelvic imbalance and poor lower back biomechanics are common in women postpartum due to changes in gravity, weight gain, and ligament relaxation. Chiropractic care postpartum provides gentle adjustments to restore normal motion in these areas, which improves recovery time. An additional benefit includes the prevention of neck, midback, and wrist pain often associated with breastfeeding and carrying an infant."

—Dr. Lisa Ortiz, Webster-Certified Chiropractor

36

*Ask
for help*

Parents, especially new ones, often feel like they have something to prove, like they need their family and friends to see that they actually can keep another human alive and happy. You have nothing to prove. If you find yourself struggling, need a break, get stuck in a bind, or want to go to brunch mimosas with your bestie, ask for help! It doesn't make you anything but a happier parent.

START WITH YOUR PARTNER

I found that getting help from my partner was the most challenging. I wanted him to have opportunities to disengage and recharge, too, but sometimes I felt overwhelmed by parenting and, at times, became resentful of his relative freedom. I found myself getting upset over things like his commute, because he got to take a nap on the train and listen to his favorite podcasts uninterrupted. Before you start going down this exhausting, resentful rabbit hole, pull back and have a frank conversation with your partner about what you both need to make this parenting jam a little more joyful. They may not even realize that you're struggling.

BE SPECIFIC

People have probably been tossing out offers to help since before you brought baby home. Sure, a lot of them use the word *help* to mean hold your baby and coo over her cuteness until she poops or spits up, but many of your friends and family members are more than happy to lend a real hand. They may just need guidance. Tell them specifically what they can do. Maybe going out feels like a chore. Ask your neighbor to stop and pick up your grocery order on the way home. Or perhaps it's the laundry that's breaking you. Ask your mom to throw in a load when she visits. There are countless small tasks you've probably been putting off that you could delegate.

IF YOU CAN'T FIND HELP, HIRE IT

Maybe you're both putting all you can into daily home and baby care. If you're overwhelmed, it may be time you outsource. Remember, help doesn't necessarily have to be baby-related. Hire a cleaning service to come once a month and take care of the heavier projects such as bathrooms and mopping, or get a neighborhood kid to mow your lawn so you have time to focus on something else. They may seem like small tasks but, piled up, they can easily start to feel like they're crushing you.

OR GET CREATIVE

If your budget doesn't allow for paying for help, it's time to get creative. Think about bartering some of what you need done. Agree to feed your brother's son or drive him to football practice for a week if he will come take care of the grass. Have a friend with a baby? Set up a baby-care swap—you can take her baby for an afternoon if she agrees to take yours for one, too.

9-12 MONTHS

37

Think about discipline

By the time you've made it to month nine, there's a pretty strong likelihood that your baby has learned the meaning of the word no. It may seem like one of her favorite words, as often as she makes you say it! Nine-month-olds are starting to enjoy their independence and learn that there are countless things to explore when parents aren't looking. It may be time to think through your discipline strategy.

Let's be honest. This is just the beginning. I'm not going to say toddler life is terrible, but you will have moments where you question your own ability to outsmart a two-year-old. Consider the things your nine-month-old is getting up to, because things will only get more, um, *interesting* from here.

Contrary to how it may feel, most child-behavior therapists would agree that your baby is largely incapable of trying to manipulate you before they hit that one-year mark. The way she sneaks up on you and flings your glasses from your face may make her appear to be a mastermind, but in reality, she's just having fun and enjoying your reaction. Young children who seem to misbehave are usually just exploring their environment and learning from the reactions they receive. Instead of going blue in the face from saying no, outsmart your evil genius with a few soft discipline techniques.

CONTAIN THE CHAOS

The fine art of containment is the easiest strategy to employ. Babies can't get into things they can't reach, and with their height deficit and lack of movement dexterity, it's easy to win this one with a few strategically placed baby gates and a playpen. Even a closed door can be your friend. Rather than saying "no" constantly, set up "yes" zones where baby *can* touch, taste, and explore everything within reach.

REDIRECT FOR SAFETY AND SANITY

Not everything can be sectioned off; sometimes baby is going to get to things you don't want her to have. When this happens, redirection is a great way to keep baby safe and you sane. Your glasses are off-limits, so offer her something she can have, like one of her toys. And while you don't need to yell "no" every time she reaches for them, a firm reminder makes sense here. There's no need to be angry or overly worked up, but you want baby to understand that there are things she can't do. Say, "You can't have Mommy's glasses, I need them to see! But how about your rattle instead? We can play with it together."

Your baby's newfound independence is a great thing! It's an opportunity for her to learn and for you to reclaim a bit of yourself in the process. You want her to be bold and confident as she interacts with her world, but you also want her to understand that there are limits. "No" is a word that is going to be a big part of your vocabulary—because sometimes it's the best way to keep her safe—but it shouldn't be the only word, or even the most frequently deployed. Get a little creative, set up a safe space, and then let her at the world so she can conquer it!

9-12 MONTHS

38

Think about weaning, or not

The American Academy of Pediatrics recommends that babies be fed breast milk or formula exclusively for the first six months. They also advise that babies continue breast milk or formula as parents begin to introduce solid foods until they reach a year old. Beyond a year, they recommend breastfeeding be left to the desire of mother and baby.

Okay, cool. Cool, cool, cool.

That's what the doctor people say, but what matters is what you and your baby say. At this point in your life, if your baby is nursing, you may be thinking about the possibility of weaning... or not! The decision of when to wean is 100 percent up to you and your baby, regardless of what anyone else has to say about it.

IF YOU WANT TO KEEP NURSING . . .

I nursed all of my children well past the 12-month mark. I enjoyed being able to spend time with them that way. They were attached to the comfort of breastfeeding—and so was I in many ways. So I didn't wean them until they decided they weren't into it anymore. Leaving the decision to them made the transition easier for us.

Nursing beyond a year was no easy feat, however. Not only was it challenging to be tied to my babies for that amount of time, but I also had to deal with the opinions of people who wanted to weigh in. When I was still nursing him at 15 months, I sometimes felt ashamed to admit it for fear of hearing negative comments.

IF YOU WANT TO STOP NURSING . . .

But maybe you're ready to be done with it—to reclaim your body and live your best life. That's cool, too. When I reached that point, the question I struggled with most was how.

For me, the key to weaning ended up being mostly about timing and comfort. First, I waited for cues from my son that he wasn't as attached to the process anymore—his feedings got shorter, and he spent more time looking around and coming off the breast to play or laugh. He was also starting to eat more table food. The day the kid decided to tear into a plate of ribs was a dead sign that breast milk was not doing it for him anymore.

It wasn't a rush job. We couldn't quit cold turkey. My kid was not trying to hear that noise and honestly, neither were my breasts. Engorgement is real, y'all! When I decided this needed to happen, he was still pretty attached to a couple of his feedings. So, I started with eliminating one feeding per day at a time. The midday session was easiest for us to kick to the curb first. He had other distractions to keep him occupied. Once that one was dead and he was taking his midday milk from a sippy cup, I decided to cut out the morning feed. He enjoyed waking up slowly, so we decided to start our mornings with a cuddle on the couch, some of his favorite books, and a sippy cup of warm milk. The extra mommy time and cuddles made the transition easier. Dad took over weekend mornings to distract him from thinking about nursing. Our biggest challenge was nighttime feeding. It took a change of routine—we went to Mimi and Papa's house for a week—to distract him. A week of falling asleep on Mimi's lap made it easier for him to forget he loved nursing before sleep.

WEANING TIPS FROM AN EXPERT

* **"Change routines:** When you get up in the morning, promptly get breakfast or start a new activity. Change the bedtime routine, replacing nursing with a song or snuggles. Sit in different spots—avoid those places that your child associates with nursing.

* **Postpone:** 'We can nurse at naptime.' 'Let's nurse after we play.' 'We can nurse when we get home.'

* **Shorten sessions:** Limit the length of your nursing sessions. You can count down, sing a special song, or use a timer.

* **Think gradually:** Pushing too much too quickly can make weaning harder. Think of weaning as a process, not a onetime event.

* **Offer alternatives:** A snack, drink, fun activity, or book could offer a distraction from nursing.

* **Don't offer, don't refuse:** This is a simple technique where you don't remind your child to nurse, but you don't refuse when they ask. It is a great way to start the weaning process with a toddler."

—*Aryn Hinton, MotherhoodMusing.com*

9-12 MONTHS

39

Sign up for a mommy-and-me (or daddy-and-me) class

Now that baby is on a more predictable schedule and parenting has fallen into more of a routine, it's a great time to sign up for a mommy-and-me class. These classes stimulate and engage your baby, and—possibly even more important—they are an opportunity to up your mom-friend game dramatically.

THEY'RE NOT JUST FOR MOMS

Dads are welcome to attend these classes with baby. They're a great way for parents to bond with baby and to meet others with children of similar ages. I found several great friends through the mommy-and-me classes I attended with my kids.

BABY BENEFITS, TOO

Parents often wonder if the classes are even worth it. Do babies learn to swim or do art or appreciate music? Your child isn't about to take one swim class at 10 months and learn to do flip turns in the pool like Michael Phelps. But courses such as swimming and music, specifically, have been found to leave baby with skills needed to become a good swimmer and appreciate music later on. Babies who take the participatory classes often learn to communicate better and become more social. Some will even pick up a few course-related skills, particularly if you continue to attend the classes over time.

THEY'RE EASY TO FIND

Wherever your interests lie—art, sports, music, dance, languages—you're probably going to be able to find a mommy-and-me class that's a good fit.

Looking for a mommy-and-me class to try? Here are a few places to start:

* Check your local YMCA for sports and movement classes for your baby.

* See if any local museums offer art classes for parents and babies.

* Local music schools, including national programs such as Kindermusik, may offer music courses for you and baby to try.

* Look for mommy-and-me classes at gymnastic centers.

* Get baby used to the water and on her way to swimming solo with a swim class. They start around six months, and, up until about age three, you will need to get into the water with your child.

* Find your zen with a mommy-and-me yoga class. These are a great fit even for very young babies and their parents.

* Visit your local public library and see if they have baby story time. This is a good way to start developing a love of reading with your children, and they're usually free!

9-12 MONTHS

40

*Take care
of your diet*

Taking care of a baby zaps your energy fast, and you need food to fuel you. A Kit Kat and a Coke aren't going to cut it, especially not if you're also trying to produce breast milk. Trying to maintain a healthy diet amid all the chaos is a challenge but not an insurmountable one.

REMEMBER, MEAL PLANNING IS YOUR FRIEND

A quick Pinterest search for "easy weeknight meal plans" can save you from spending hours trying to come up with something for dinner other than tacos. You can search for and pin the recipes to a secret board while you're feeding baby. Plan to make enough for leftovers at lunchtime, and then you just have to think about breakfast and snacks.

BREAK YOUR FAST WITH SOMETHING HEALTHY

For breakfast, steel-cut oatmeal topped with almonds and fresh strawberries or bananas is a great option. Cook your oats overnight in your slow cooker and enjoy them in the morning. They're easy to store in the refrigerator and reheat each morning. Here are a few other things to try.

* **Breakfast toasts:** Start with your favorite whole-grain bread and cover it with mashed avocado and a fried egg, nut butter and bananas, or even ricotta, pears, and honey.

* **Smoothies:** For a filling option, start with plain or vanilla Greek yogurt, and then add the fruits, veggies, or grains you like most. Good combos include bananas with uncooked oats, almond milk, cinnamon, and nutmeg; oranges, vanilla, and honey; and spinach, mangoes, and bananas. Think about getting a blender with a single-serve option—the Oster My Blend 250-watt blender with travel sports bottle is an economical choice—so you don't have to bother with too much cleanup.

* **Baked goods:** Baked ahead and filled with healthy, hearty ingredients, these are a great grab-and-go option. I love quinoa muffins with carrots or apples for a great start to the morning.

SIMPLIFY GROCERY SHOPPING

There are few things more joyful than grocery delivery. It shaves off tons of time, and putting on real pants is avoided entirely. If you're too much of a procrastinator to take advantage of delivery options, lots of stores offer pickup options, where grocery fairies come out and put your order into your trunk. Added bonus: You'll save cash by not wasting money on impulse buys.

TRY A MEAL-ORDER SERVICE

If you can make time to throw together a meal in 30 minutes or less, a meal-delivery service option may be a good fit. Meals are delivered to your home, ready to cook with an easy-to-follow recipe included. There are several options available. Here are a few I've tried:

* **HelloFresh.** Hassle-free meals with familiar ingredients prepped and ready to cook. They provide a ton of variety in their weekly menu options, including a family plan and a veggie plan. They also make it easy for those with allergies to enjoy their meals.

* **Home Chef.** They offer 38 chef-designed meal kits each week, so there is plenty of variety. They also allow substitutions and additions to make your meals more suitable to your tastes or dietary needs. They even have five-minute lunch and oven-ready options.

* **EveryPlate.** They consider themselves "America's most affordable meal plan" and keep costs low by only offering eight meal options per week. They still offer fresh ingredients, are ready to cook, and come with easy-to-follow, 30-minute recipes.

41

Capture your memories

You've probably heard parents say, "The first year is a blur." I see no lies! There are moments, weeks, months possibly, from the first year with my boys that have dropped from my brain. Maybe I blocked some of it out for the sake of my sanity, but there were times when I was going through the motions of living life at a pace my brain could not keep up with.

I cherish every instant with my children. The first smile, the first laugh, the first time my son peed directly into my smiling mouth while I changed his diaper. They're all special, memorable moments in different ways. But it's overwhelming at times, and it's often challenging to tell your brain to remember something that you may want to look back on one day. That's why journaling became so important for me.

I've always loved to write, but it's a joy I lost when I was in the throes of new parenting. I didn't have time to journal about my feelings before bedtime each night.

Eventually, as I eased into my parenting gig a bit more, I started to jot down notes about my feelings, my thoughts, things I wanted to Google, things I wanted to remember. It became a sort of on-the-go baby book where I chronicled our lives. These entries weren't written to be shared. There were no thoughtful prompts to inspire them. They were just musings about the moments I shared with my baby and reflections about what they meant to me. The entries are brief, but they're honest in a way I don't think they would've been if I'd been writing it for him to read one day. Instead, this is a gift to future me that I'll probably read through and sob over when he graduates from high school.

There are many ways to capture your memories of this time:

* **Start a memory box.** Toss in small things you want to hang on to. Maybe keep a table of contents and write a bit about each one when you add it so you remember why it was important at the time.

* **Write annual letters to baby.** Some people start this before baby is born, but it's never too late to start. Pen a letter to baby about your lives this year. Share the joys and the struggles along with your hopes for the future, too.

* **Record a video journal.** Writing's not your jam? Think about recording solo videos and one together as a family each year.

* **Keep a journal.** Daily, weekly, monthly, it doesn't matter. Whatever feels right, do that. And it doesn't have to be just about baby. It's your journal, too, so make it about whatever feels good to you.

* **Start a 365 baby-and-me photo project.** Commit to taking a picture with your baby each day. You may not appreciate it now, but one day you will, and so will your baby.

GET IN THE FRAME

"Moms are only too happy to point our cameras and phones at our kids. But rarely are we in the photos. We have every excuse in the book as to why we are not there: My hair is not done, I don't have on makeup, there is dried-up food on my shirt. EXCUSES! When our kids are 30 or 40 or 50 years old, they won't care that our hair wasn't perfect that day. But they will have that photo of the two of you together. They will have a photo of the love that shines through your eyes as you look at them. They will see you all TOGETHER at Disney. TOGETHER at the park. TOGETHER in random moments. That's priceless. So, get in the photo! Hand off your camera, turn the selfie camera on yourself. Leave evidence that you were there, too."

—LaShawn Wiltz, everydayeyecandy.com

42

Reignite your style

We can all agree that it makes sense, especially in the early days of motherhood, to fall into your favorite comfy pants and ratty college tee daily. No matter what you wear, it's probably just going to get messy anyway. Plus, it pays to stay nap-ready at all times. But it's also easy to lose yourself to that couch life. Before you know it, you're getting whisked away to New York City for a makeover on reality TV.

At least that's what happened to me. Caught in the doldrums of what had become my sweatpants-clad mom life, I found myself surrounded by family, friends, and two of America's most popular stylists, Stacy London and Clinton Kelly, as they begged me to say adios to my fleece-covered existence once and for all. My appearance on *What Not to Wear* in 2011 was courtesy of my BFF, who'd had enough of me going to the swimming pool in sweats. Fortunately, the producers saw potential in me, did a surprise ambush, and took me to New York for a head-to-toe makeover while millions of viewers watched.

The experience taught me a lot about loving myself for who I am in the moment, appreciating my body for the amazing lives it has created, and discovering that being a mom doesn't mean that I'm not still a lot of other amazing things, too. I also learned the true meaning of "look good, feel good" and the power a well-fitting dress and a killer haircut can bring.

DON'T LOSE YOU

It's easy to lose yourself a bit after you become a mom. Your body might be different, your lifestyle may shift, and finding clothing that fits the new you can be frustrating and exhausting. While investing in a brand-new postpartum wardrobe is neither feasible nor advisable for most of us, it's worthwhile to find what makes you look good and feel great, too.

IF YOU CAN'T GET ON REALITY TV . . .

Stacy and Clinton may not be able to crash your closet, but that doesn't mean working with a personal stylist is out of the question. Companies like StitchFix, Wantable, Trunk Club, and several others make personal stylists accessible to many more women (and men, too!) looking for style guidance. A short style-preference quiz and a small styling fee are all it takes to get you started. Letting a style-savvy person hand-select a few chic pieces for me to try on in my own home sure beats trekking to Marshalls, kid in tow.

Not ready to get outside help? Mom style blogs might be the answer. TheMomEdit.com, RattlesandHeels.com, and TakeTimeforStyle.com are a few I've been reading for years. I check their posts and follow them on Instagram for daily style inspiration.

43

Embrace your new body

I struggled with this. There are many days that I still struggle with this. The weight gain, the stretch marks, the floppy bits, the loose skin—I beat myself up daily after I had my first baby … and my second … and my third because of the changes my body had gone through. I was desperate to regain some semblance of my old self after giving birth, and I was focused on the physical parts. It caused me to lose sight of what mattered when it came to my post-partum body: I was healthy and capable of enjoying my baby. Time spent lamenting the loss of your perky breasts and flat belly is time spent not enjoying your baby. Don't let concern for things that don't matter interfere with growing a meaningful life that does.

But getting there can be tough. Changes in perspective and behavior may be the key to helping you embrace your postpartum body so you can live your best life in the skin you're in.

UNDERSTAND DIFFERENT ISN'T NECESSARILY BAD

The body you're in right now may be different from the body you were rocking a year ago. It's also a body that has proven its capacity for greatness. Think of the beautiful creature it created from a simple ball of cells. It nourished her, protected her, and pushed her into this life where you can hold her and sniff her neck and kiss her toes to your heart's content. Think of the warmth, comfort, and safety this body provides to that same little person who loves every square inch of it. Appreciate her; she's a goddess.

REMEMBER IT'S NOT PERMANENT

The body you're in right now, or even 10 months from now, is not a prison. It will change. You can change it. Maybe you'll decide to adjust your diet, increase your fitness, or get pregnant again and have even more babies to love. There's no reason to spend time loathing something that could be on a new path tomorrow.

DON'T LET IT HOLD YOU BACK

You're healthy, you're capable, you're happy, and you're alive. You may not be loving some of the remnants of pregnancy that are hanging about your bones, so focus on what you do love, and live for those things. Go out and play with your baby. Go to the pool and splash around with them. Walk with them, run with them, soak them up. When you're living a full, active life, you're happier and more able to make healthy decisions. But give yourself time and grace. Give your baby and your partner and your friends the attention you've been giving your waistline. I'm certain you will be a happier human and your body will look it.

GIVE YOURSELF PERMISSION TO MAKE A CHANGE

So, you've decided this isn't the body that makes you feel the way you want. You can't move how you want to move or enjoy what you want to enjoy, and you feel limited and unhappy with where you are. Fine. I get it. We all want to be healthy, and if making a change is what will allow you to get there, then get it, girl. Making a change, however, requires commitment and sacrifice. You want to work out more so you can get stronger? Awesome! You'll also need to give yourself permission to dedicate time and effort to that. You want to alter your diet so you're eating more nutritionally sound foods that will help your body reach its optimal performance level? Cool! You'll have to allow for that in your budget, maybe change where you shop, and devote a little time to meal planning. If this is something that is important to you, then unapologetically devote yourself to making it happen. Push aside the mom guilt and any other excuses. You deserve to feel amazing in your skin, and if physical fitness is what you need to make that happen, then do you.

9-12 MONTHS

44

Trust your instincts

*A*dvice. You've probably been getting it since the day you announced your pregnancy. While some of it is useful, the vast majority of it makes you fake smile and roll your eyes internally. It's not likely to stop once baby makes her appearance. You'll be counseled on everything from how to dress her to college savings plans from those you love and trust and from perfect strangers, too.

DON'T LET IT INTERFERE WITH YOUR INSTINCTS

They're real, they're yours, and they deserve your respect. One day they could totally save your baby's life. When Grandma pops by and tells you that your baby looks fine even though you know, deep in your heart of hearts, that something is wrong, *trust that*! You're not going to hurt yourself or your baby by erring on the side of caution, and you need to get into the habit of trusting your gut. It's unlikely to steer you wrong.

ASSUME POSITIVE INTENT

This sage advice comes from one of my oldest and most cherished friends, Liza Hawkins from (a)MusingFoodie.com. Along with inspiring delicious meals for my table, she also inspired me to adopt this attitude toward most people I encounter—assume positive intent. It basically means that you allow each individual interaction to stand alone and never assume someone, with no history of such behavior, is acting nefariously. It has allowed me to salvage several relationships while preventing me from looking like a tool by incorrectly judging someone. When it comes to parenting advice, this attitude works well. Most people sharing this advice, unsolicited though it may be, are coming from a place of care and kindness. They generally believe they're correct, and they want to be the answer to whatever problem they think you have. They may be completely off base and misinformed, but that doesn't make them evil or even deserving of your discontent. Smile and nod and do whatever you were planning to do anyway.

STAND UP FOR YOUR CHOICES WHEN YOU NEED TO

Most of the time you can let the unwanted advice roll off your back, but every now and then, you have to bring the hammer. If you've got someone pressuring you and pushing negativity into your life, it's time to let them know you're not here for that. You have every right to raise your baby without input or interference from anyone, and yes, that includes your mom, your partner's mom, your coworker, and anyone else who has something to say about the choices you're making for your baby and yourself.

9-12 MONTHS

45

Book a couple's getaway

*Y*ou've nearly made it through your first year of parenting. You've earned yourself a getaway! Grab your partner or your bestie—or just your bag if you're flying solo—and book a weekend away, sans baby. It doesn't have to be super involved, expensive, or extravagant…but it totally can be!

There's something to be said about disconnecting from work and home responsibilities, and maybe even from your digital life, to focus on your partner. It feels right to take time away to remember how you got here and maybe even practice a little for the next go-round without worrying about being interrupted by your child.

So, book it! Don't let mom guilt or dad guilt or any guilt get in the way. You may have to be creative with timing (maybe the weekend Grandma arrives for her two-week visit?), budget (camping, anyone?), and even destination (you've always wanted to visit the B&B two towns over, right?), but a weekend away is a weekend away, especially when you're with your person.

Once you've got your travel plans in order, your mother-in-law is scheduled to stay with the baby, and you're headed to the airport, it's time to relax and focus on soaking up every moment of your baby-free getaway. Try a few of these things to make sure it's as refreshing as you've hoped.

HOLD HANDS

They're probably full most of the time at home. This is your chance to put them on each other a little more instead of baby and all of their accoutrements.

TALK ABOUT WHATEVER THE HECK YOU WANT

Lots of people recommend keeping the kids out of the conversation, and while I see value in maybe putting some limits on yourself, I also understand the impact these little people have on every facet of your life. Not allowing yourself to talk about them is like not allowing yourself to think with your brain or feel with your heart. Plus, my husband and I enjoy telling tales of our experiences with the kids, sharing things the other missed while away at work, reminiscing about hilarious or cute moments. If you and your partner want to talk about your baby, *talk about your baby*. You want to feel good and enjoy each other, not spend the entire time trying to avoid the baby elephant in the room.

BUT LEAVE THE STRESSFUL TOPICS FOR LATER

This may be the most focused face time you and your partner have had in months; don't waste it going over your retirement savings options. You could probably hash that out via email when you get home. The same goes for work woes, home-related responsibilities, and all of the day-to-day things that make your head spin. The whole point of this getaway is to leave your worries behind for a couple of days. The only thing that should be making your head spin is the delicious wine you're enjoying while you wait for your massage to begin.

PUT THE PHONES AWAY

Listen, I love taking photos as much—okay fine, *more*—than the next gal, so I'd never say you have to go phone-free to enjoy your vacation. You'll want to snap a few baby-free pics of you and your partner, and your sanity will also require daily baby check-ins. But don't spend more time looking at your phone than you do looking at your partner. Promise each other no work calls, no emails, and no social media while you're away. Use that time to catch up on the things caring for baby caused you to push aside this past year.

9-12 MONTHS

46

Get your affairs in order

Did you know that for babies born in 2018, the average American will spend about $232,000 raising a child from birth to age 17? If your child is born after that, you can expect to spend even more. Thank you, inflation. This is one of the most expensive investments you will ever make, and while the ROI is priceless, it gets you thinking about whether you've taken care of the adult stuff when it comes to your finances.

There are so many things to think about when you welcome a new family member: health insurance, life insurance, savings plans, investments, taxes, and countless other considerations. Your best bet will be to get yourself to a professional. Find a reputable, certified financial planner who can advise you on how to make sure you and your baby have secure financial futures. Regardless of where your income level is, this is an important first step. Those with less financial security will probably benefit most from taking the time to learn about the best ways to manage their income while also discovering viable opportunities to increase it.

In addition to the money, it's important that you think about what will happen to your children if you and their other parent pass away before they turn 18. In your heart you may know that your sister is going to take your babies and love them like her own, but the courts don't know that unless you tell them. You can save a lot of time, turmoil, and money for your family members and your children if you name a guardian for your children in your will.

FAMILY FINANCE TIPS

"While it can be one of the less exciting parts of welcoming a new child, there are a few things that you should do to ensure that your family finances are in good order.

* Review all insurances; most important: life, health, and disability.

* Within the first year, consider establishing a 529 College Savings Plan. These funds grow and are distributed tax-free when used for qualified educational expenses.

* Review and adjust your household budget as necessary. Plan to conduct a more regular review of your recurring and one-off expenses.

* Review your will and beneficiary designations. If something were to happen to you and your spouse, having your wishes for your child and your money spelled out officially is a good idea.

Something that you should not do is buy life insurance on your newborn child. Regardless of what anyone tells you, there is never a reason for life insurance on a newborn."

—Shabri Moore, CFP®, AIF®, CDFA®, Moore Wealth

47

Do a cake smash photo shoot

One of the trendiest things to do right now for baby's first birthday is a cake smash. It sounds like something super adventurous, but it's really just your baby and a pretty cake (or another delicious food item she's probably experienced) that she gets to eat with her hands while having her photo taken. I highly recommend planning one of these to commemorate your baby's first year. It will be a fun way to say goodbye to infanthood.

The great thing about cake smash photos is that they're easy to set up. They don't require much preparation on your part aside from securing a cake. You can hire a professional photographer to capture the experience, but even if that's not in your budget, grabbing a few great pics of your baby living her best life with cake smashed all over her birthday face is totally worth it.

If you're planning a smash photo session with your birthday baby, here are some things to help you make it a success:

DECIDE WHAT YOU'LL HAVE BABY SMASH

The original idea of a first birthday smash involved baby destroying a beautifully made first-birthday cake with her hands and face. It's fun to get a gorgeous cake to take pre-smash birthday photos with, and then allow baby to go to town for the smash photos.

Some more creative parents with personal food obsessions like to have baby smash something other than a cake. Fun options include tacos, avocados, and barbecue. If you're a family with a food you love, you might want to give that a try. It's more fun if you stick to something baby can actually sink her hands into and get all over her face, but what to smash is entirely up to you.

HIRE A PHOTOGRAPHER

Or not. This is one of those things you can easily do on your own if a photo session isn't in your budget right now. A pro will come with lots of props and great ideas to bring your vision to life, but even with your camera phone and a pair of extra hands, you can create an amazing first-birthday smash session that costs nothing more than the time it takes to bake a cake.

SET UP A SMASH-PROOF LOCATION

If weather permits, outside—preferably within reach of a hose—is going to be your best bet. As you've probably seen, babies tend to wreck shop when they go in on their cakes, so you'll want to make sure it's not happening on the family-room carpet.

If you do need to be inside, make sure you start with a don't-care-if-it-gets-ruined base layer. It's best if you can toss it when you're done, but an old sheet or towel will work fine. If you are going for a more styled shoot, go to your local craft store and buy a yard of fabric to match your theme. Even a big piece of white butcher paper will work.

MAKE IT FANCY

You may be going for a simple cake-on-a-high-chair vibe and that's totally cool, but you can easily turn your baby's first-birthday-cake-smash session into something viral-worthy with a few fun additions. If you have a theme, create a backdrop and add props to match. For example, if you're a Disney family, get a Mickey or Minnie Mouse cake, dress baby in their best Mickey- or Minnie-inspired attire, and then add mouse ears and other Disney touches to make a magically memorable shoot.

HAVE A BLAST

This is a celebration, after all, for baby and for you! You want this to be a fun experience all around. There's no need to stress about making it perfect. It's the imperfection of a cake smash that makes it so beautiful.

48

Find a hobby

Or go back to one you gave up when the whirlwind of pregnancy took over.

When parenthood sets in, it's easy for your interests and activities to revolve entirely around baby, but this is a dangerous path to travel down unless you enjoy the idea of one day finding yourself home alone, stalking your teenager on Life 360 because her social life is more exciting than yours. Your new role as a parent may supersede some of the other roles you used to play, but that doesn't mean it should erase them. Think about things you previously enjoyed doing, the things that fulfilled you, brought you joy, challenged you, or made you a happier person, and think about how you might include them in your life as a parent.

HELP YOUR BRAIN AND MAYBE YOUR WALLET

Having a hobby to escape to from time to time can be extremely beneficial to parents and their children. They're a great way to relieve stress. They may help you develop new skills or increase your knowledge. My hobby—writing my blog—eventually grew into my full-time career, allowing me to generate a healthy income to help support our family. You never know how giving yourself time to be creative and curious or to explore something exciting might pay off. If nothing else, you can rest assured that it will benefit your mental health. Studies have shown that adults who engage in creative activities or physical recreation each week report significantly better mental health than those who do not. So, if you won't do it for yourself, do it for your kids. They deserve the healthiest parents possible, right?

TRY SOMETHING NEW—TOGETHER

If you didn't have many hobbies before baby, now might be the time to think about finding one. If nothing else, it's a good excuse to sneak in a little me time . . . or a little couple time.

If you're looking for a way to connect with your partner, a hobby you can both enjoy, such as starting a garden or hiking, might be the way to go. You can bring baby along, or you can reserve it for times when you can sneak away. When my middle son was a baby, my husband and I decided to start playing tennis together. Neither of us had played much before, but it was simple enough to pick up quickly, and it was a great way to get outside and enjoy active time together. Playing together also helped us reach some of our health and fitness goals—and the fun of a little friendly competition didn't hurt either.

Making time for activities that are not baby-centered is challenging but also important to your individual wellness and your relationship. Start by committing one hour to your hobby each week. Put it on your calendar. Handle it during naptime or lunch time if you must—just make it happen so you can see how good it can be for your mood, productivity, and well-being.

Need ideas for hobbies you could pursue without much experience? Here are a few that won't break your budget or take up much of your time:

* Grow a container or herb garden

* Write in your journal

* Take photos of something you enjoy looking at that isn't your baby

* Sign up for a dance class

* Register for a 5k and then start training for it

* Start a blog

* Try geocaching

* Explore a new individual sport, like swimming or golfing

* Make over a piece of furniture

* Try to learn a new language

9-12 MONTHS

49

Learn to save money

*A*dding a new family member is expensive. From the moment you find out you're expecting until your child graduates from high school and beyond, you're going to be racking up the bills. Food, clothing, housing costs, day care and school, insurance, medical bills, so many things. That said, there are countless ways to save money on day-to-day things that could greatly reduce your baby-raising bill over time.

GET YOUR MEDICAL INSURANCE COMPANY TO PAY FOR YOUR BREAST PUMP

Did you know that the government requires most insurance plans to pay for breastfeeding support and supplies? That means you may be able to get your breast pump for free. Contact your insurance provider to find out if you qualify.

VISIT CONSIGNMENT SALES AND SHOPS

You can save on lightly used goods, such as strollers and clothing. Babies grow out of things so quickly it makes sense not to buy them new unless you have to. Bonus awesome: You can make money by reselling your stuff at these locations, too.

One thing you should go ahead and purchase new is a car seat. You want to buy new so you can make sure it has the latest safety features, has never been in a crash, hasn't been involved in any recalls, and includes all of the attachments and directions that came with the seat. Buying it new in the box from someone who didn't use it? Fine. Buying it out of the back of some moving van at the flea market or on your neighborhood swap page? Not so much.

GO TO YARD SALES

Or use Facebook yard sale groups in your community. You can do all of your shopping without driving all over town and hoping to stumble across something decent. If your town doesn't have a specific group for baby or child items, consider starting one yourself.

USE AN ONLINE THRIFT STORE LIKE THREDUP

This is the largest kids' consignment store and thrift shop online specializing in secondhand clothing. Their baby and kids' sections are pretty legit, and you can find tons of things for discount prices.

TAKE ADVANTAGE OF TARGET'S CAR SEAT TRADE-IN PROGRAM

Annually, since 2016, Target has offered parents coupons for 20 percent off new car seats and booster seats when they bring their old car seats in. Visit Corporate.Target.com or Google "Target's car seat trade-in program" to find out when the next event is.

DIY YOUR BABY FOOD

Jarred baby food is a convenience item that saves you time but costs you money. You can make healthy and delicious baby food right in your own kitchen, and you don't even need any special supplies to do it.

USE A FLEXIBLE SPENDING ACCOUNT TO PAY FOR CHILDCARE

If your employer provides this benefit, you may be able to fund a dependent-care flexible spending account that allows you to put a certain amount of your income aside, pretax, to reimburse your family's childcare costs. There are a number of rules and possible tax implications for going this route, so be sure to speak to a tax professional or accountant before you get started.

50

Celebrate baby's first birthday

*T*ime to get your party on! Baby is one, and it's time to celebrate! It may seem like yesterday that you were being wheeled out of the hospital in the community wheelchair, with baby tucked into her carrier, and yet here you are with a one-year-old. Time sure flies when you're having fun. Or when you're exhausted from chasing your toddler around the house. But the big day is finally here, and it's time to plan a celebration.

First-birthday parties have become a big deal. From setting up an entire carnival with a petting zoo and pony rides in the backyard to renting out beautiful venues, the one-year-old birthday party has almost become what the Super Sweet 16 was in the early 2000s. But as with many things, there's no one right way to do this, and you don't have to feel pressured to go all out for the big day. This celebration is as much for you as it is for baby, so make it something that will allow you both to enjoy the day with those who love you.

A few considerations to keep in mind before you start blowing out that candle:

YOUR BABY HAS ZERO EXPECTATIONS

Whatever you want to do to celebrate will be A-OK with baby. There's no need to throw a Pinterest-worthy party your first time out. If all you did was hug your baby, she would be fine with that, so celebrate in a way that feels right. Leave the handcrafted balloon archways to the Kardashians.

BABIES DON'T CARE WHO'S ON THE GUEST LIST

The guests are there for you, mostly. Don't worry about inviting baby's "friends" from day care or the mommy-and-me swim class.

ENCOURAGE DONATIONS IN LIEU OF GIFTS

It's a great opportunity to encourage people to donate to a cause you and your family are passionate about and avoid spending a bunch of time trying to exchange double gifts and things that don't fit.

MIND THE SCHEDULE

Don't punish yourself by scheduling the birthday party in the middle of naptime, or right before bedtime. The day is already going to be overwhelming for baby, and she may even round it out with her first sugar high. She's going to need that nap to make it through all the excitement, and compromising bedtime is not the way to end a happy day. Also, keep it short. Two hours is going to feel like an eternity to you and baby if you have a house full of guests to entertain.

IF YOU'RE HOSTING A BIG SHINDIG, THINK ABOUT A SEPARATE CELEBRATION FOR CLOSE FAMILY

Bigger parties with lots of guests make it challenging to celebrate with the people closest to you and baby. Think about hosting a small dinner party on a different night where you can give the most important people a chance to celebrate with baby. If that means you, your partner, and baby go out to dinner and sing over a lit cupcake at Outback, then so be it.

Epilogue:
So, What Now?

You're feeling like a boss now that you've made it through year one of parenting. Your kid is probably sleeping more predictably, eating more foods, and starting to do big-kid things like walk and talk and enjoy being out and about. Or not. Regardless, you're on your way to a new adventure in year two. Your baby will definitely master that walking thing, start communicating more with words, and maybe even do super-fun things like climb on tabletops and beg to get out of the cart in Target. So, keep your running shoes laced as you head into year two.

A FEW THINGS TO EXPECT THIS YEAR:

* **Everybody and their mother is going to start asking you when you're going to give your baby a sibling.** It's none of their business, and it's rude to ask, but they're going to anyway. Get yourself a standard answer and dole it out to everyone who weighs in on your procreation. Maybe you've already decided that you're a one-and-done kind of family. Cool. Feel free to let them know that you're happy with your family the way it is. If you're still deciding, or you and your partner are struggling with infertility, or secondary infertility—the inability to get pregnant and/or carry a child following a pregnancy—like more than three million women in America, this could be a touchy subject. Ask a loved one to spread the word so you're not bombarded with questions at every family get-together.

* **Your baby is going to start talking, and possibly never stop.** It's so cool when you finally get to hear what your kids are thinking, and as they near the end of year two, most children will have a pretty hearty vocabulary. They may even be stringing together words to make sentences. Don't be alarmed, though, if your child isn't super talkative. If your one-year-old is vocalizing sounds and using gestures to communicate her wants and is able to follow directions, she's probably right on track. Bring any concerns you have to your next visit to the pediatrician to be on the safe side.

* **Lots of independence.** Your baby is going to become quite the little do-it-herselfer this year. Expect her catchphrase to be "I do it!" and expect her to mean it. It's awesome to see your baby climbing into her car seat alone and buckling herself in. It's less awesome when you're already eight minutes late for your doctor's appointment and still *need* to go through the Dunkin' drive-through to get an iced coffee.

* **Lots of hugs and open-mouth kisses.** Toddlers love love—hugs, kisses, cuddles . . . your two-year-old will be here for all of it. They may not understand "pucker up" yet, though, so get ready for lots of juicy, open-mouth kisses all over you face.

Here's wishing you another amazing year! Get ready—it's going to be a big one!

Resources

I'm not the only parent to listen to when it comes to making your life more fun, simple, and amazing. Check out these websites and blogs written by and for parents that can help you create a little bit of awesome in your day-to-day life with baby.

WEBSITES & BLOGS

EverydayFamily.com
This is a community of parents who share advice and information as well as guidance and support for every step of your parenting journey. You can find everything from baby-name tools to real-life stories about life with a preemie right on the site.

EverydayEyeCandy.com
This blog, owned by a wonderful friend of mine, LaShawn Wiltz, is a great place to go for photography inspiration, tips, tricks, tutorials, and courses. She will help you learn how to take seriously 'gram-worthy pics of all of baby's most beautiful moments while reminding you to come from behind the camera to be a part of the story, too.

RedTricycle.com
The national site runs as a blog offering parents advice, information, product recommendations, and entertainment, while the local editions provide more specific info on things to do in your neck of the woods. The Bump + Baby edition is a great resource for new and expectant parents.

HowToBeADad.com
My favorite place to get the dad perspective on things and lol at funny posts and memes on dad life, husband life, and life in general.

PostpartumProgress.com
The most informative, supportive, and positive resource for maternal mental health and wellness I've seen.

La Leche League (llli.org)

If you need to find a lactation consultant near you, look under "Get Help," and then "Find Local Support" on their homepage. You may also want to join their Facebook support group, included below.

BabyQuip.com

For renting baby gear when you travel so you don't have to haul it yourself. It's a pretty genius idea. Also, if you're looking for a way to make a little change on the side, you can sign up to be a gear provider and rent out some of your own baby gear.

FACEBOOK GROUPS FOR PARENTS

I have found Facebook groups to be a wealth of support and information throughout my parenting journey. If you're active on that platform, type the name listed below in the search bar to locate the group.

Breastfeeding support: La Leche League Breastfeeding Support

Based on due date: Just type "Due Date Group" into the search bar and look for the month your baby was/will be born.

General mom support: New Moms, Moms-to-Be, and Experienced Moms

General dad support: A Bunch of Dads

Dads only: NEW DADS PLACE, a *Dads Only* Supportive Dads Group

Buying and selling baby/toddler goods: Momma | Baby | Toddler Buy Sell Trade

Moms of boys looking to connect with other boy moms: Boymom Squad (#lifewithboys group for moms of boys)

Dads of daughters: Dads With Daughters - We Are All On A Journey of Discovery

Parents of kids with special needs: Special Needs Parents Support & Discussion Group

APPS FOR NEW PARENTS

White Noise Deep: Say goodbye to sleepless nights and fussy babies. I actually used this often with a baby I nannied a few years ago, and it was awesome. Works magically for older kids and adults who struggle to get to sleep, too.

Baby Tracker – Newborn Log: One place to keep track of everything baby—nursing, wet and soiled diapers, sleep, wake times, growth. They have a photo album and ways to track baby's firsts. You can also share among caretakers.

Wolf + Friends: A community for women raising special-needs children. You can connect with others, get advice, read informative content, and even get local-practitioner recommendations.

Snapseed: If you love creating Instagram-worthy pics, this photo editor app does it all and is super easy to use.

Babypics: Speaking of photos, this app has all of those fun overlays you see on photos that allow you to keep track of baby's growth and share what they're up to.

Peanut: An app for like-minded moms to connect. It allows you to find nearby moms for playdates and meetups.

WHERE YOU CAN FIND IN-PERSON MEETUPS

Finding local groups for parents to meet in person helps make the transition to parenthood much easier and way more fun. These sites and apps offer opportunities to interact with other parents who are in the same stage as you, and they may be where you meet your future mom-life bestie.

MochaMoms.org: Support group for mothers of color with local chapters across the nation. Any and all are welcome to join.

Mops.com: It technically stands for Moms of Preschoolers, but all moms with young babies are welcome, and you will often find lots of parents with newborns in your local group.

MomsClub.com: This group is specifically designed for at-home mothers. Their mission includes moms who work at home, work part-time, own businesses, or work at family businesses, but their goal is to support those moms who are spending a good chunk of their day at home with their children to help make this experience less isolating.

Fit4Mom.com: They are the company that owns Stroller Strides, a total-body-workout fitness option for moms with babies in strollers that meets in local cities and is led by an instructor. They also own Stroller Barre and several other fitness courses that are hosted locally.

AtHomeDad.org: Provides support for stay-at-home dads, including a listing of local dad groups across the nation.

Index

Acknowledgments

Thank-yous are my least-favorite part of stuff like this, not because I don't know how to thank people, but because I am super anxious I'm going to forget to thank someone who helped me along this journey.

I know I have to start with Mimi. My mom was the first person in my life to think I could do something like write a real-life book. She dreamed about it before I even dreamed about it. Believed it before I even believed it. This is the first thing I've ever written that she wasn't the first to read. She would've loved to see my name on the cover of a book, and I am so sad that she missed this. I'm sure she's telling all of the angels about it up in Heaven.

I also need to thank all of my dudes—my husband, Paul, and my sons, Tony, Will, and Alex—for giving me the time and support to make this happen. Thank goodness Chik-fil-A was more than willing to take all of my money in exchange for their delicious chicken sandwiches and waffle fries.

To my bestie, Vanessa Mahone-Garcia, thank you for reading every chapter of this book and telling me which parts were awesome and which parts weren't. To my dad, Lawrence Self, I appreciate you always being so proud of what I'm doing even if you don't always understand it, and to my little brother, Matthew Self, thank you for thinking I'm the best writer on the face of the planet even if you never actually came out and said it—I could tell you were thinking it.

Last but not least, I want to thank everyone who has read DudeMom.com or found me on the DudeMom Facebook page and left a comment, sent a message, or tracked me down at the football field to say something I wrote made them laugh (or smile, or cry). You are the reason I continue to write stories and share funny moments and open my heart and our lives to share with others. Thank you, thank you, thank you.

About the Author

Amanda Rodriguez is the founder of *DudeMom*, a blog where she chronicles her busy, on-the-go life raising her three sons. You can find Amanda's writing about parenting on well-known sites such as ScaryMommy, HuffPost, Redbook, NFL, and more. She has been featured on the *Today Show*, was an original iVoices video creator for iVillage, and has also appeared on unscripted shows on both TLC and Nickelodeon.

Amanda met her husband, Paul, at UC Irvine in Southern California. Today they are the proud parents of Tony, Will, and Alex, whom they raise, along with their two dogs, Maya and CoCo, in western Maryland. When not writing, helping clients design awesome digital-marketing strategies, or working as the marketing specialist for the Frederick County Chamber of Commerce, Amanda spends her time volunteering with one of the youth-sports organizations her sons belong to, watching vampire shows, and eating tacos. She's decided to sleep when she's dead.

CPSIA information can be obtained
at www.ICGtesting.com
Printed in the USA
LVHW010622171219
640683LV00001B/1

9 781641 529143